FANATICISM

FANATICISM

A Psychological Analysis

Josef Rudin

Translated by
ELISABETH REINECKE AND
PAUL C. BAILEY, C.S.C.

UNIVERSITY OF NOTRE DAME PRESS
Notre Dame   London

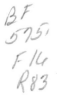

Contents

Contents

Introduction

I. THE PROBLEM

1. Fanaticism as a Universal Problem

In all likelihood there has never been a period in the thousands of years of the history of the human race which is unacquainted with the fanatic and has not experienced and suffered outbreaks of blind, raging fanaticism. Entire ethnic groups have for a shorter or longer time been swept up by the lava of fanatic eruptions. In such situations religious, political, and social revolutions have had an almost instantaneous power to draw the

1

sluggish, slow-moving masses into their wake, stirring up their dormant tendencies toward extreme and radical claims and attitudes. The picture of the history of the human race from the first primitive tribes and nations even up to our present day as a constant war between races, ethnic groups, and various classes is clear evidence that intolerance, aggression, nihilating tendencies, and destructive instincts are motivating forces of man's existence-struggle and are taken as a matter of course— so much so that man can hardly envision his own existence without the factor of war. The best efforts of man have not yet succeeded in eliminating the world-historied and primordial fact of war as being an unnecessary and detrimental means of interhuman relationships. This evidence sheds enough light on the human situation to allow us to see into the psychic attitude which is the object of our study: fanaticism.

Racial, geographical, and climatic differences carry no weight here; at the most they can only delineate a more precise formation of the fanatic countenance. Alongside the cruel features of notorious Asiatic fanaticism we see the burning fanatic faces of Slavic conspirators and nihilistic revolutionaries; we meet the passionate temperaments of the Mediterranean and Latin American types; we recall the horrible scenes of the Spanish civil war and of never-ending revolutions. Yet these are in close kinship with the somewhat paler, thick-blooded, and gloomy, introverted Nordic fanatic who less often stages politico-social revolutions but instead destroys and blows up his inner world with fanatic probing (Ibsen, Strindberg, Kierkegaard, and so on).

Neither does sexual differentiation protect one from fanatic behavior. Together with Savonarola, Calvin, Robespierre, Lenin, Hitler, Castro, and numerous noisome and aggressive as well as quiet and tenacious male fanatics we find—intellectually on a completely different level, yet quite comparable in their fanaticism—the nuns of Port-Royal, the furious women of the Halls of Paris, the emancipated bluestockings and the angry proponents of woman's rights, climaxing in the female commanders of the concentration camps of our own time (Ilse Koch) who are armed with whip and revolver. They all join hands through the centuries in their radical attitude and unyielding warfare, in their real or imagined rectitude in defense of their ideas and convictions.

There is hardly any profession in which fanaticism does not tend to smolder and here and there suddenly burst into flame. Even in the quiet realms of scientific activity, more often than the layman would suppose, we find disputes carried on with no less intrigue and cold fanatic calculation than are found in the religious wars and social revolutions of past and present. It is not an exaggeration to say that every scientific and technical achievement is quickly grabbed up and put into the service of political aims, social claims, and religious convictions.

Finally, it is a rare individual who is completely safe from the fanatical attacks emerging out of his own unconscious psyche. Certain phases of life incite even the most peace-loving citizens to exhibit a remarkable receptibility to fanatic judgments and positions. It is not only the adolescent puritan who can be carried away by the fervor of a new idea; even in the second half of life a person can suddenly catch fire for some absurd goal and become a warrior—and even old age can still show passion in its half-closed eyes and once more burst into flame. Dostoevski's nearly ninety-year-old Grand Inquisitor paces time and again not only through the history of the world and of the Church but also through the streets of our small towns, raising his voice in city hall council chambers. Thus fanaticism seems to be a quite general possibility of human behavior and a universal problem.

2. Fanaticism as a Problem of Our Time

To the extent that modern man is not indoctrinated by totalitarian ideologies he is still largely co-formed by ideas of enlightenment, rationalism, liberalism, individualism, and philosophico-religious relativism and likes to envision himself as being immune to the intolerance of former times. With a certain tone of superiority he speaks of the religious fanaticism of primitive peoples and the bloody Aztec cults, and of medieval cathedrals as "monuments of fanaticism." Yet, without being aware of it, he thereby merely joins other fanatics—for instance

those of the French Revolution who demanded the destruction of these "monuments of fanaticism," and consequently, according to the official protocol 235, the
statues of the Strassburg cathedrals were destroyed.[1] Our
day, which has proclaimed respect for external and internal personal freedom as the Magna Charta of its profession, has believed itself incapable of falling victim to
a one-sided, opaque fanaticism. The facts speak differently. Totalitarian political systems with their hecatombs
of victims of cold-blooded terror and the labor and concentration camps of Siberia, Tibet, and Auschwitz have
again brought to our awareness how little the human
psyche actually changes and how strong are certain
psychic tendencies which lurk about, waiting for an
opportunity to break out. Political and social intolerance
have taken the place of religious and philosophical intolerance. Man's urge to represent something absolute
seems ineradicable. C. G. Jung once said: "There is in the
psyche some superior power, and if it is not consciously
a god, it is the 'belly' at least, in St. Paul's words."[2] One
can also be a fanatic apostle of vegetarianism!

Whenever this urge for the absolute is repressed and
man "modestly" renounces all certitude and clarity, even
in regard to ultimate questions, he may be willing and
also capable of tolerating for a longer period of time
hundreds of opinions and contradictory convictions, but
finally someday this attitude becomes unbearable. The
loss of absolutely valid truths and values generally

pushes him into a psychic unshelteredness and instability
which delivers him up to the power of irrational unconscious tendencies and lets him fall victim to the magic of
extremes: fanaticism. Then that which "pure" reason has
thrown into the street as garbage is all the more assiduously smuggled back in through the gate of practical
reason.

We cannot overemphasize the fact that the abandoning
of objectively obligatory values and of their hierarchy
leads to an increase of the subjective values of experience which is often confused with an "existential attitude." The values of subjective intensity and individual
achievement take the place of suprapersonal values
which have become questionable. Hans Sedlmayr, in his
book *Der Verlust der Mitte*, much discussed because of
its leaning toward the established order, has designated
two characteristics typical of today's life-feel and form-
drive which lead into the very proximity of fanaticism:
on the one hand radical purism (pure painting, pure
architecture, pure objectivity, pure science, purely religious questions, pure race, monocultures) and, on the
other hand, polarization, tending to separate opposites
to the degree of irreconciliability and even of contradiction (reason *or* feeling, intellect *or* instinct, intellect as
enemy of the psyche, knowledge *or* faith, historicism *or*
vision of the future, conservation of culture *or* starting
from scratch, individualism *or* collectivism). Thus the

valid value-yardsticks of the center have been replaced by fascinating yet simultaneously fanaticizing extremes. The intensity of subjective experience becomes the ersatz for lost absolute values and must constantly be increased and overheated to fanatical degrees.

The loss of ultimate, valid positions in respect to ideologies also plays a part in the explicitly transitional character of our time, which most people somehow sense and which pushes them all the more into the unrest and insecurity that favors fanatic short circuits and intolerant behavior as solutions.

Yet even if we disregard the clearly evident demonstrations of a sometimes consciously instigated fanaticism, there are still those greater and lesser forms of an exaggerated and feverish attitude typical of our times which we so much tend to repress but which a generation to come will probably recklessly uncover and hold against us: fanaticisms of achievement, speed, record-setting, every year demanding victims of human lives and of general health. These, by the way, are excrescences that can lead to most serious aggressive behavior.

Thus we by no means believe that our age with its high level of general education and its relativism in regard to ideological questions is protected against new outbreaks of fanatical ideas, but, on the contrary, we consider it just as much in danger of the multiple forms of fanaticism as were former times.

3. FANATICISM AS A PSYCHIC PROBLEM

A phenomenon so universal as fanaticism is necessarily multifaceted. From the *historical* viewpoint the question arises: What historical situations are especially susceptible to mass epidemics of fanaticism? Let us call to mind the critical periods of the Middle Ages when hunger and plague ran rampant and in their wake witchcraft and the persecution of the Jews reached new heights. It is also legitimate to ask whether periods of too rigidly established order constricting human life may not provoke a fanatic tendency toward freedom. From the *ethicoscientific* viewpoint the question of fanaticism leads to complicated discussions concerning the moral justification or condemnation of fanaticism. What should be the judgment of a philosopher of ethics when Plato has maintained that art is always created only "in a state of rage" and when a psychiatrist even more acquainted with the problem of fanaticism says, "The most impressive and heroic deeds of world history, the imperishable and most valuable achievements in art and science would be unthinkable without the stimulus of fanaticism"?[3] When even the simple man on the street, on being questioned, will answer, "Fanaticism has something good about it, it is somehow necessary,"[4] a clarification is urgently needed. In this context it may be well to call to mind the lengthy and sometimes violent disputes between ethical rigorism, tutiorism, probabiliorism, equiprobabilism, and probabilism within Catholic moral science.[5] Finally, a *sociology* of fanaticism would have to point out significant insights into the social preconditions, especially, of the origins and development of mass fanaticism.

The aim of our book is to shed light on fanaticism as a *psychic* phenomenon. The questions here arising are manifold. The manifestations of fanaticism, its different forms, will have to be distinguished and described; the psychic conditions causing fanatic kinds of behavior must be brought to focus. Is it the psychic constitution, the inner structure, which is the determining factor of fanaticism? Do Kretschmer's schizothymic and Jaensch's J^3-type perhaps have a special inclination for fanatic behavior? Or is fanaticism a resultant peculiarity, in the sense of G. Pfahler, which is developed in a certain type (of a close and tenacious attention-set) only when, simultaneously, a violent resistance from the outside makes itself felt? Does fanaticism originate as compensation for one's own inner insecurity, as C. G. Jung emphasizes: "Fanaticism is the brother of doubt"? Yet perhaps it can also be maintained that man becomes a victim of fanaticism only when educational and environmental influences have guided him into radicalism and intolerance, or when psychic disturbances of a neurotic or a somewhat psychotic nature have unbalanced his psychic equilibrium.

Finally we must take into account the psychic and organic side-phenomena of fanaticism: the intensity of

affect, the rigid orientation of thinking, the hard inflexibility of will, the mechanization of the imaginal and
perceptual tracks, the acceleration of breathing, the
inhibited or exaggerated language of gestures, the fervent
or frozen sound of the voice, the sullen gleem of the
eyes, and so forth. It is even reasonable to ask whether
fanaticism cannot take over and mold a person to such
an extent that we must see this fanaticism as an essential
part of this psychic core and so must also include the
effects fanaticism has on his other psychic energies of
structure-forms as well as its influence on the proximate
and remote environment.

The prolixity of these questions may indicate to us
how tight is the integration-coherence within the psyche
and how far-reaching are its effects. A psychic phenomenon such as fanaticism can be understood only when seen
in the plethora of these psychic contexts, backgrounds,
and conditions.

II. CONCEPT AND METHOD

1. USE OF THE TERM AND CONCEPT

The term fanaticism is surprisingly often put to use,
especially in its adjectival form. In everyday conversation
it is quite common to designate as fanatic individuals or
entire groups as well as many forms of human expression
and action in almost all areas of life and culture. One
speaks of fanatic zealots for religious, political, national,
social, scientific, or artistic causes and at the same time
of fanatic abstainers, vegetarians, sportsmen, mountain-

climbers, hunters, hobbyists, chess-players, jazz fans, collectors of stamps and shrunken heads. We are acquainted with fanatic moralists, self-torturing ethical perfectionists, fanatics of cleanliness (with their symptoms of compulsive washing), fanatics of order and detail, fanatic bureaucrats, and also those "bohemians" who are fanatic enemies of all pedantry. There are fanatic existentialists and fanatically narrow-minded citizens. We admire or chuckle at the fanatic lovers who jump off the bridge in their grief, and we despise the fanatic tyrants who unscrupulously sacrifice millions to their will-to-power. At times the fanatic is a blindly raging prophet and iconoclast who destroys irreplaceable works of art or is an inquisitor who burns the enemies of holy faith in an auto-da-fé; at other times he is the one who with quiet and stubborn tenacity lives day and night for his invention. Sometimes he is a selfless friend of the poor and abandoned, consuming himself in his heroic urge for self-sacrifice. Is it not confusing to speak of the fanatic charity of Tolstoi, Pestalozzi, and Albert Schweitzer in the same breath with the fanaticism of Savonarola, Calvin, and Robespierre?

The face of fanaticism shows so many features that it is difficult to see and comprehend them from a single psychic background or from a single psychic focal point. Can we, in spite of this, trust in the "genius of language" and surmise that in all these cases people have something in common in their psychic attitudes?

To call someone "fanatic" demands responsible judgment. After a little thought we may prefer terms such as exaggerated, one-sided, passionate, fervent, stubborn, obstinate, daredevil, headstrong, narrow-minded, dogged, intolerant, aggressive, relentless, unyielding, monomanic, cruel. The fact that often there are many words to adequately replace the term fanatic should arouse suspicion that it is often used rashly and inexactly, and also that fanatic behavior is not a quite simple but rather a very complex psychic process. Yet in view of this broad use of the term we may now point to an important peculiarity which must be taken into consideration when discussing the problem of fanaticism: The term fanatic is used not only for those figures who entered history as typical fanatics and whose entire psychic profile seems to be co-formed and intrinsically permeated by fanaticism, but also for those individual traits of a man's character which can exist alongside other, perhaps equally characteristic, qualities. In the first case fanaticism is psychically central, belongs to the core and gestalt of the person, while in the second case it appears as a more or less significant, marginal, peculiarity.

The *concept* of fanaticism is derived from the Latin word *fanum,* which means the sacred, the beneficial, the salvific, the temple, the consecrated place. The term *fanaticus* is already found in Latin literature and there means: to be put into a raging enthusiasm by a deity (*Wörterbuch Georges*). Cicero uses the term also for the secular realm: "isti philosophi paene fanatici," and in

Seneca it is even used as a verb, *fanari,* "to rage." In German the term hardly appears before the eighteenth century and fanatics are at first seen as "raging fighters for religious principles" (Kluge-Göthe, *Etymologisches Wörterbuch der deutschen Sprache,* Berlin, 1951). An expansion of the concept occurred under the French influence when the Camisards in their political fight were called fanatics.

In a psychological analysis of fanaticism one might from the start—a priori, so to speak—try to define fanatic behavior so clearly as to distinguish it from all other types of behavior undeserving of such odium. But the questionability of such an arbitrary definition of the concept becomes immediately evident.[6] Without doubt, the inductive method is necessarily wearisome and lengthy when one takes into account the many and various manifestations labeled fanatic and tries to come, by degrees, to a legitimate definition of fanaticism freed of nonessential components. In this regard we should not forget that the psychological method of concept-formation, in contradistinction to the philosophical, proceeds mainly through emphasis rather than through definition.[7] Finally we would like to make it crystal clear that we do not wish to be hairsplitting concepts and terms but that we are attempting to shed a little light on psychic facts in order to more fully comprehend the psychic situation called fanatic in view of its extensive background.

2. Method

There are at least as many psychological methods as there are psychological schools. There are the philosophical-understanding-phenomenological schools (in which there is hardly agreement as to the meaning of phenomenological); there is the descriptive method—questionnaires and tests—and there is the analytical method. It is not our intent to use, let alone prescribe, any one of these methods exclusively but rather to seek in our own way to psychically illuminate and psychologically explain the entire scope and span, the many contexts and backgrounds of our encounter with whatever is called fanaticism.

This demands at least a partial justification. It would be easy and perhaps also very promising to consider fanaticism from the viewpoint of depth psychology. The doctrine of psychic energy would give us a very convincing picture of fanaticism as a complex of psychic energy. Not often can we see the buildup of psychic energies so clearly. Moreover the hermeneutic possibilities of depth psychology in regard to fanatic types of behavior would very often be in order, since fanaticism is also a first-rank problem of the instincts, and hence repressions, overcompensations, unconscious identifications (for example, in the form of an exaggerated sense of being "chosen" displayed by some fanatics), and naive projections on the "enemy" play an extremely great role. The psychotherapist probably meets fanaticism most frequently in the form of perfectionism and ethical rigorism and, let us add, with all its aggressive tendencies even to the point of murderous and suicidal impulses. One may also be tempted at times to think that every neurotic has fanatic traits since his fixation implies at least an unconscious absolutizing connected with compulsive mechanisms and aggressions.[8] In some cases fanatic behavior can also be interpreted as a desperate attempt to break out of an infantile situation into an object-world.

Despite this, we do not proceed by the method of depth psychology, but choose our own approach because it seems important and legitimate that we try to open up the problem from as broad a starting position as possible and to see fanaticism from the very beginning not simply from the neurotic and pathological viewpoint. Then, if depth psychology comes to the fore by itself in most cases to provide us with explanations, it will be all the more convincing. Besides, when we deal with the famous historic personages of fanaticism we lack an important and indispensable material of the unconscious: a sufficient number of dreams, phantasies, drawings, and paintings. Of course, this material could be worked out in part through a formal analysis of style, for instance, a study of the letters and sermons of Calvin and Savonarola. But this would require a very sophisticated psychological knowledge of style.

Even though we do not intend to follow a specific

method, our procedure will be mainly phenomenological (in the most general sense of an illumination of
the nature from the immediately given) with bypaths
into philosophical-understanding and depth-psychological
methods. Herewith three aspects have shown themselves
as essential, leading to further questions and to the possibility of bringing the phenomenon of fanaticism on a
broad scale into the psychological viewpoint:

   I. Fanaticism as a problem of intensity.
  II. Fanaticism as a problem of value-attitude.
 III. Fanaticism as a problem of pathology.

These three aspects interpenetrate one another. The
first indicates the strongly subjective state of the fanatic,
which is so obvious, especially to the onlooker. The second aspect brings into focus the confrontation of this
condition with various values and their repercussions on
the subjective psychic attitude; thus it emphasizes the
self-knowledge of the fanatic. The third aspect seeks to
clarify the pathological component in that it deals above
all with the compulsively mechanistic, instinctive reactions of the fanatic. The first two of these aspects are
founded on the supposition that every psychic event in
man follows the laws of psychic energy but can also be
co-formed by the freedom of the psychic value-attitude.
The third aspect deals with the disturbance both of the
subjective state of the arranged "energy-household" and
of the value-attitude (and their interaction). Therefore

it seems hardly promising to consider fanaticism only as psychic disturbance, since this disturbance must be viewed as belonging to borderline cases where the subjective state as well as the objective value-influence must play a role in our understanding. Our procedure, sensitive to such differentiation, can be justified only by its results. We are convinced that the clarification of a psychic behavior from these three aspects is justified, since it is also truly anthropological. Therefore, let us angle in on the phenomenon of fanaticism from these three viewpoints in order to see and interpret it with a greater span of comprehension.

Obviously, in using examples of personages from the history of the world, of the Church, and of art, we are necessarily susceptible to subjective viewpoints and judgments, and hence we do not intend to present a new, let alone final, interpretation of these figures but are interested only in a clear insight into the fanatic components of their behavior. To what extent historical persons have been distorted by the "parties of favor and opposition" and misrepresented through psychic prejudices and projections can be determined only by a strictly historical investigation. Our purpose is not historiography but the clarification and understanding of psychic events and their characteristics.

Here we may call to mind two confessions of Nietzsche, the first of which was written in a sketch of a "preamble" to his *Dawn of Day* together with the warn-

ing not to read his newest thought "without circumspec-
tion": "When I recently undertook to reacquaint myself
with my earlier writings which I had forgotten, I was
alarmed by a characteristic common to all of them: they
speak the language of fanaticism. In almost every place
where something is said concerning those who have
other convictions the bloody kind of slander and mali-
cious enthusiasm that are signs of fanaticism become
noticeable—ugly signs which would have prevented me
from carrying through my reading to the finish had the
author been only a little less known to me. Fanaticism
spoils character, taste, and simultaneously also one's
health, and whoever wishes to recover all three must be
prepared for a lengthy treatment."[9] Later on, however,
the same intellectually keen Nietzsche says of himself:
"In vain does one look for a fanatic trait in my nature."
(*Ecce homo:* Why am I so clever?) Thus what we are
interested in here cannot be judgments about historical
personages but solely a more comprehensive and perhaps deeper knowledge of the universal phenomenon:
fanaticism.

CHAPTER ONE

Fanaticism as a Problem of Intensity

I. INTENSITY AS A QUANTITATIVE CATEGORY

What first catches our eye when we deal with fanatic individuals, groups, and movements as well as with fanatic behavior and forms of expression is intensity. By "intensity" we wish to express here the degree of energy with which one lives, feels, thinks, wills, works, and in general confronts the objective world, and, more exactly, a degree that works at top speed. In all fanatics this enhanced and even superenhanced intensity is not only conspicuous but is a characteristic sign constituting the fanatic, so to speak. It therefore seems reasonable

that we first view fanaticism as belonging to the category
of intensity. The limits of such a view and the resulting
dissatisfaction will force us to resort later to further
categories of understanding.

The intensity we meet here is a quantitative category.
Positively, it indicates a certain degree of energy, energy-
unfolding, vitality, liveliness. Negatively, it represents
the quantitative viewpoint which ignores consideration
of value. Of course, fanaticism can never get started
except in view of some value. Mere "chemically" pure
intensity would, as we know, not only be a loss of conscious value-goals but also the unconscious abolition of
all guiding instincts, the lack of all archetypal images,
and the absence of even the most minimal value-experiences. Such a "pure" intensity seems scarcely ever to
manifest itself in the concrete life-situation. But the
intensity of the zealot can shift so much into the foreground that the cherished value itself slides into the
background and is no longer truly and deeply experienced but becomes shallow and even falsified. It is possible that from the very beginning there was not a
significant value-experience. Here we recognize the
"little" fanatics who stubbornly fight, in a blind rage, for
something that they themselves have experienced only
superficially and with hardly any depth. But it can also
be that in the course of an intensive struggle an originally
significant value-experience has gradually receded and
become secondary and has even been slowly "devalu-

ated" until it is completely lost or even twisted into its opposite; after decades of struggle one may no longer know the reason why he at first began to fight. The fighting instincts and mechanisms have increased in intensity while, at the same time, the original goals and values have become obsolete. This confirms the old fact of experience: the more intense one is, the less he is selective of ends and means.[1] The dynamics usurp the law of action.

To what extent this is at least in part an unconscious process could be determined only by depth analysis. On the other side, however, that which causes the deep and serious problem of the "great" fanatics is the very fact that the dialectic of intensity and value-experience continues within them and almost tears them apart. "Everything I touch becomes light, everything I let go of, coal; I am certainly fire" (Nietzsche). This is a striking formulation of the tragedy of Dionysian intoxication; intensity and value may initially go hand in hand and help each other, but then comes the moment when they are in conflict, the moment when man must freely decide whether the intensity in its whirlwind is losing the value or whether the value itself and the will for value can control the intensity. We will deal more thoroughly with this conflict between intensity and value in the chapter concerning fanaticism as a problem of value-attitude.

Intensity as quantitative category allows for a large scale of measurement: There are varying degrees of vehemence strongly contrasting with one another which can be differentiated in the individual fanatic event as a gradual or quick, even a sudden increase and, likewise, as various gradations of decrease and even sudden cessation.

Moreover intensity as quantitative category manifests itself in *two directions:* toward the outside as a loud and excited, strongly aggressive, and at times destructive discharge of energy; toward the inside as a silent, mild-tenacious, rigid-inelastic, doggedly stubborn energy buildup, as an innermost concentration and fixation upon an ideal. Fanaticism in this second case is by no means weaker than in the first and not only shows similar forms of expression, such as tightened body movements and constricted gestures, but can also come to the point of similar desperate destructive tendencies. Whereas the outward-directed fanatic finally seeks to destroy his environment, the inward-directed has denied his environment from the very start, has liquidated it in his innermost depths, and allows it to exist merely at the margin—excepting, of course, the one lone value which he has permitted to exist.

Finally, psychic intensity as quantitative category can have its roots in different psychic "layers" out of which it is discharged in such a way that there can be seen three *forms* of this intensity which are essential in this context of fanaticism. These forms are encountered as excitement, passion, and rage of will. We often meet these forms interconnected, yet a clear predominance of one of the three is not infrequent. As a result more distinctions in fanatic behavior become visible and this makes possible a further clarification of the phenomenon of fanaticism; therefore a separate handling of these three forms seems to be in order. After this we still have to consider the equally important problem of the psychic background of these forms of fanatic intensity.

II. FORMS OF FANATIC INTENSITY

1. FANATIC EXCITEMENT

We speak of excitement as an event which can originate in the psychic realm but which then quickly takes hold of the somatic area of expression and sets especially this area into vehement vibration. With mounting interaction excitement can then continue "psycho-somatically." Fanatic excitement manifests itself primarily in the body "layer." It is this layer-specificity that determines almost by necessity the *concrete manifestation* of fanatic excitement.

First and foremost the especially sensitive organs and functions of the body may vibrate, shake, tremble, quiver, and kick up. Excitement then manifests itself as a specific agitation or tenseness, even as a constriction of the body muscles and of the gestures (for instance, a clenching of the fist or stiffening of the fingers). It is evident in the fixed gaze or in the restlessly rolling eyes, in the sharpening of the voice, in shouting and yelling, or perhaps merely in "grandiloquent diction," which is so commonly referred to in psychiatric literature. It may also take the form of an extremely accelerated, or in some rare cases even painfully slow, manner of speaking. This tenseness takes hold of individual parts or even of the entire motor system and gives the impression of an inhibited or almost completely paralyzed motility. At times it lets go with unexpected suddenness, be it in a reaction of the whole body, in violent striking movements, trembling, quivering, or in a sudden "collapse."

The excitement of the fanatic seems to manifest itself toward the outside as "explosions," eruptions, elemental violence, frenzy, fits of rage, or as an outbreak of heretofore silenced or repressed judgments, feelings, and emotions. Think of Adolf Hitler's fits of rage when he not only shouted at rulers of foreign countries and the highest generals of the German army but even personally tore off the insignia of rank of these generals or at times bit into his fist or a rug.[2] But excitement can also turn inward and affect one's vitals, as an increase of the entire "tonus" of the world of mood and feeling, as an altered sense of vitality, whether it be pleasurable feelings, satisfaction, and a sense of victory or feelings of displeasure due to the resistance of one's environment. Above all, however, it is a powerful exertion of the entire psychophysical apparatus.

Not all fanatics produce such states of excitement as a form of intensity. A poorly integrated type of fanatic is able to separate and split his dully glowing passion or rage of will from the more strongly somatic-conditioned excitement. Some of these belong to the split-personality type. Yet in most fanatics a more or less pronounced excitement is generally noticeable.

Neither is this form of intensity manifested only in the more strongly "structure-given" fanatics in whom it always remains latent and lurking, but especially also it can be seen in those surprising fanatic outbursts of individuals who for the rest seem less susceptible to fanatic behavior. For excitement is strongly tied up with the moment and after a sudden upsurge it often just as suddenly ceases, or in the case of a maximal saturation it can turn into the opposite, into apathy or acts of remorse.

We meet the state of fanatic excitement in both the little fanatics of whatever type of conviction and in the great fanatic geniuses. But its "pure" form is seen mainly in the little fanatics, while in the fanatic geniuses it is generally combined with other forms. Of six thoroughly investigated cases of eccentric fanatics in the psychiatric clinic of the University of Breslau all evidenced this state of excitement, either as a constant general irritability or at least as an affect-laden excitement when proposing certain ideas. These six cases were representative of a relatively moderate fanaticism (conscientious objectors) —simple, professional people who for the rest did not seem to be extremely irritable but rather quite correct, quiet, and polite individuals.[3] One of these cases, H., who was treated by Kujath, was ordinarily a rather rigid, reserved, fearful fanatic. He is reported to have created quite agitated episodes: "Within the family he demanded absolute consideration. The slightest change of routine at home set him into emotional outburst. In view of the extreme sensitivity of his nature one had to carefully weigh beforehand the effect of anything that was said to him."[4]

In some fanatic geniuses the state of excitement manifests itself at high pressure, in combination with passion and rage of will, for instance in fanatic work-intoxication. Here excitement may at times be so powerful that we may legitimately give this phenomenon of excitement special emphasis. Many examples of this extreme inner excitement with all the characteristics of the external excitement can be found in every history of art and literature. True, some of these personages cannot simply be called fanatics, but at the same time it can hardly be denied that a fanatic tendency, apparent only in a state of excitement, is clearly recognizable. Flaubert "when he was working acted as though he were insane. He would sit day and night over a manuscript drying his sweat or his tears, and, like Schiller, he recited aloud, sometimes shouting, the dialogue of his characters, often needing hours to complete a single sentence. He hated Madame Bovary as a demon enslaving him and he tasted the arsenic which she used to poison herself so clearly on his tongue that he had to vomit."[5] Similar things can be said of Balzac, Turgenev, and many others.

Nolde writes in his autobiography: "I painted and painted, scarcely knowing whether it was day or night, whether I was a human being or merely a painter."[6] Kokoschka's biographer thus describes the artist at work: "With feverish hands, wildly and painfully he throws the paint unto the canvas in a Dionysian excitement that makes one breathless in amazement and terror before the abysses of human yearning and salvation agony."[7] Kafka, in a similar state of frenzy, wrote his great novel *The Judgment* between ten o'clock in the evening and six in the morning. Throughout his entire life Van Gogh was an excited man, whether he was proclaiming Christ's joyful message to the mineworkers in the Borinage or whether later on he was turning out his paintings in an overexcited state—paintings evidencing all the convulsions and flare-ups of their master. At times he squeezed the color from the tube directly on the canvas.

Finally, the highest degrees of excitement are seen in the "famous" fanatics. Concerning Savonarola, Pastor, by no means an unfavorable biographer, says: "He raged in the pulpit in a manner bordering on the insane."[8] He also used "a language whose violence was unusual even for that time. Geiler von Kaisersberg, his contemporary, preached in the Strassburg cathedral and unquestionably gave bishops and canons a piece of his mind, still he did not surpass all limits as did Savonarola."[9] We are also acquainted with Calvin's terrifying excitability; every detail put him into rage. Doumerque recounts: "On the occasion when he failed to find certain documents he assumed that they had been stolen and his anger was such that he had to stay in bed next morning and could not go out until the evening."[10]

Part of the characteristic of increased agitation is that it often spills over into the surroundings and can at times even *"contaminate"* the masses with its radiation. Sementovsky, who takes pains to place Savonarola in the company of the prophets, says of the sermons of Savonarola: "Many women and sometimes men fell into crying spells during the sermon while others remained mute and motionless as though paralyzed by horror."[11] Yet it is equally characteristic for this transmission of excitement to quickly collapse and even to turn into its opposite when the exalted preacher does not appear on the scene. This is also reported by Sementovsky. Similar emotional contaminations accompanied by the wildest excitement are described in regard to the *collegia pietatis* of the pietists, in which ecstasies, prophecies, speaking in tongues, spasms of repentance, and states of maniacal screaming at times fell the listeners like an epidemic. The "convulsionaries of St. Médard" in Paris in the years 1731 to 1732 were even more grotesque: "You saw, in the cemetery, 'men falling like epileptics, others swallowing pebbles, glass, and even live coals, women walking feet in air. . . . You heard nothing but groaning, singing, shrieking, whistling, declaiming, prophesying, caterwauling.' 'Women and girls, who played a great part in these exhibitions, excelled in capers, in somersaults, in feats of suppleness. Some of them twirled round on their feet with the lightning quickness of dervishes; others turned head over heels, or stood on their hands in such a way that their heels almost touched their shoulders.' On the tomb itself you saw the Abbé Bécheraud, hopping incessantly on one leg, and proclaiming that his other leg, which was 14 inches shorter, was growing by a ligne every three months. 'There were nearly a hundred, of all ages and sexes. You could spend a whole day waiting in a queue to reach the tomb itself.' "[12]

The transference of fanatic excitement to large masses has been long recognized, but even today it is still not possible to prevent such contaminations despite the investigations concerning mass psychology. The Middle Ages had their dancing frenzy, especially in times of pestilence and epidemics, but we too should wonder why even today states of mass excitement can bring our young people to the verge of ecstasy; for instance, rock-and-roll groups, the "new sound," can cause thousands to shiver and shake in fanatic excitement.

We cannot close this section dealing with excitement in the form of fanatic intensity without at least mentioning its counterform, paralysis. The statement that extremes touch each other is most true in regard to fanaticism. In fact, excitement and paralysis are side by side and alternate with especial clarity in the fanatic. (The two reflex mechanisms, storm of movement and

feigned-death reflex, alternate in a similar manner).
Fanatic excitement presupposes a great lability which,
as we know, is caused by the lack of a true elasticity and
of adaptive capability and breaks out whenever the
fanatic feels his "system," his "method," or his "idea"
to be in peril. Rigid, masklike behavior is part and parcel
of the one-track mentality of the fanatic, of the uniform-
ity of his thinking, and the narrowness of his field of
vision. This rigidity turns into excitement whenever his
system or idea is attacked, only to return again to an
inflexible attitude, a psychic armor and a hedgehog-
position. The banal and primitive complete identification
with a system first dries up and kills the inner vitality
so that the rigidity, the interior blocking and masklike
behavior are merely an expression of this life-hostile
identification, and then excitement in its exaggerated
form indicates a deeper untenability of the inner situation: The place of living dialogue has been taken over
by the deathly dialectic of paralysis and overexcitement.

2. Fanatic Passion

If we disregard the integration-coherence of the
psyche and for the moment do not take into consideration its possible combination with the other two forms
of fanatic intensity, we can say that fanatic passion has
its roots in the layer of the vital instincts and the feelings.
Against Wellek, who wants to see all fanaticism as
"merely instinctive and instinct-determined,"[13] we argue

that even though there is an instinctive and instinct-determined fanaticism, this is only *one* form, to be seen alongside the others. Likewise we differ with Pfahler, who would make a high emotional susceptibility the basic condition of fanatic behavior,[14] in that he, too, sees only a single form of fanaticism and does not sufficiently recognize especially the third form in its different layer-specificity, which we shall deal with later on. Here when we speak of fanatic passion, we recognize and intend to show that what Wellek and Pfahler understand as fanaticism is only one of several forms. While the intensity of excitement does not necessarily imply fanatic traits in every case—since, as we know, other emotions, such as fear and joy, can also cause strong excitement—it seems in contrast that a great passion is hardly thinkable without at least here and there a fanatic tendency. Such a tendency can coerce an individual into fanatic behavior if he does not succeed at building passion into his entire personality-structure and in ennobling it.

The layer-specificity of fanatic passion must be clearly kept in mind if we are to understand its *concrete manifestation*. It is through the fusion of instinct and affect that passion receives its complex character: an active dynamics on the one side and on the other the passive yet long-lasting emotional condition. The instinct's contribution is vehemence, impetuosity, and impulsiveness, qualities that can accompany the aforementioned excitement but can also exist without it. What is above all

instinct-conditioned and at the same time instinct-
enhancing is fanatic passion's blindness, or at least its
fatal simplification and reduction of reality and its gen-
eralization of the particular situation.

In 1495 Savonarola said in a sermon: "You are all
corrupt, in your speaking and in your being silent, in
your acting and non-acting, in your belief and your
denial. . . . Everything of our time is only vanity, everything is hypocrisy."[15] This he said in Florence where for
years he himself had strongly influenced the way of life!
In his sermon of February 18, 1498, he called his enemies "godless people and devils."

Thomas Müntzer, the Anabaptist, makes similar simplifications and generalizations in regard to the primitive
Church: "After the death of the disciples of the Apostles
the immaculate virginal Church through spiritual adul-
tery became a whore because of the learned. . . . Then
came the unchaste woman in her red skirt, the blood-
shedder, the Roman Church, disagreeing with all other
churches and thinking that her ceremonies and gestures,
pieced together out of paganism, were the best and all
others a shocking atrocity." And he threw similar simplifications also at Luther in his angry writing "against the
spiritless [!] soft flesh in Wittenberg." Müntzer opposes
justification based merely on faith without works and
accuses the reformer of Wittenberg of seeking to pacify
the despairing consciences of the Christians with false
consolations, saying that Luther's teaching makes "all

Christianity sincerity an abomination." He scoffs at the by no means soft Luther, calling him "brother softy and father tiptoe."[16]

In a simplifying way naive ideas of reform are elevated into personal life-ideas: "The egotism of man must stop . . . people must give up their salaries . . . only the State should have income, it must take care of everyone . . ." says Huber, a teacher, a schizoid fanatic whom Alexander von Muralt describes at length in his book *Wahnsinniger oder Prophet?*[17]

How blinded by instinct, unguided by any logical deliberation, and unhindered by doubt this passionate intensity of fanaticism can be is shown also by the example of Carry Nation during the prohibition era in the United States. She became a virtual pioneer against alcoholism, battled excited, unruly mobs in the saloons, and smashed everything she could lay hands on. She had no regard for the loss suffered by the owners. Her inspiration was her husband, who drank himself to death shortly after their marriage. She did not put the blame for this tragedy on the lack of control or pathological disposition of her husband but rather on alcohol.[18]

Of course the question arises whether in a particular case it is primarily the instinct that leads to one-tracked thinking, simplifications, and generalizations, or whether, conversely, it is a specific kind of thinking which gives more latitude for the instinctive behavior. For instance, Walter Nigg says that Calvin "found it difficult to under-

stand the opinion of someone else. He did not have the
capacity of identifying with another person and he rashly
considered alien ideas devilish."[19] Without doubt, a
strongly fixated attitude of thought (in the meaning of
Pfahler's typology) furthers the absolutizing tendencies
and provides them with more instinctual energy, but it
is also a fact that the instinct-laden impulses necessarily
narrow down even more the intellectual angle of vision
and let in only a small section of reality. Thus we must
assume that an interaction takes place.

Still, the concrete manifestation of fanatic passion
is determined not only by the instinctual component but
also receives essential traits from the area of the *feelings*.
Some authors disagree with our position, but it seems to
us that this is because they are not willing to see different
forms of fanatic intensity. Pfahler, for instance: "If coldness and callousness took the place of the high emotion-
ality, fanaticism from the very start would be deprived
of its innermost exciting factor."[20] To the contrary,
Wellek emphasizes: "Fanaticism is therefore at best
'blind passion,' not true passion, and even unfavorably
distinguished from blind passion by its coldness and
rigor, very much in contrast, for example, to the blind
passion of love."[21] Kujath, too, lays stress in the case of
H. on a "cordoning off of the emotional."[22]

This contradiction is resolved when we point out that
in fanatic passion fortissimo feelings necessarily play a
part, whereas, as we see it, the fanatic rage of will causes

these feeling-tones to lapse into silence, which explains the coldness and rigor. Kretschmer solves this problem convincingly. He finds fanaticism mainly in the schizoid types and derives the tenacity and cruelty of the fanatic from his structure-given emotional coldness, but at the same time he recognizes the ambivalence of the schizoids, who are simultaneously hypersensitive and cold,[23] and notices in them the absence of "affective moderation."[24] In our context, however, it is true that without the participation of the feelings there is no fanatic passion! Only the feelings can bring man into that state of emotion and enthusiasm and arouse in him the high temperature of fervent ardor that breaks out in a "holy anger," a blazing fury which generally destroys but once in a while can also be constructive. "Fanaticism originates primarily in our affect-life. The indwelling passion impulsively urges fanaticism into action and gives it power," as Horstmann so rightly observes.[25] This is why the most horrible deeds and crimes can spring out of this fanatic passion which finally gives vent blindly and unrestrainedly to its fury in obsessive delusion. In March, 1823, in the lowlands of Zurich, Margaretha von Wildenbuch forced her relatives to crucify her an hour after she had cruelly beaten her sister to death in a fanatic religious delusion.[26] Here, of course, we come to the borderline where the intensity of fanatic passion takes on pathological forms and leads to paranoid delusional ideas and uncontrollable impulses.

Wellek's idea that the blind passion of fanaticism "is very much in contrast to the blind passion of love" suggests to us the contrary idea that even the blind passion of love at times shows very strange traits which seem not very remote from fanatic qualities. Are not vehement expressions of love rather quickly combined with sadistic and masochistic actions? Aggression and tenderness have a surprising affinity, as Hans Kunz has thoroughly proved.[27] Think of the most ordinary caresses, such as the kiss which not infrequently turns into a bite. Furthermore, spurned love and sexual orgies turn into hatred and aggression, and even into destructive tendencies. Beautiful Eros becomes a raging demon of destruction. Does not the figure of Cleopatra, as well as her imitators, display fanatic traits? Neither is the gluttonous, dreamy passion of the *Werther*-epoch by any means without such traits.

Not every passionate exuberance, however, should be suspect of fanaticism. Let us strongly emphasize that there is a passion which not only belongs to healthy psychic behavior but which is rightly called noble since it ennobles man and gives him dignity. It must not be confused with fanaticism. Whenever there is a complete absence of this healthy and noble passion man slips more and more into a shallow, fearful, and narrowminded attitude that avoids all risks. It goes on without intrinsic, personally acquired conviction, without strongly independent initiative, and without burning enthusiasm in a weary and sterile indifference, contenting itself with mere perceptions and cunning note-taking, and at best exhausts itself with clever judgments and loses all creative capacity. Nietzsche says to this boring, resigned kind of person: "Oh, that you would become cocky; oh, if you would still have convictions!" We may also call to mind the words of scripture: "I would that thou wert cold or hot. But because thou art lukewarm, and neither cold nor hot, I am about to vomit thee out of my mouth" (Apoc. 3:15).

What the Greeks call apatheia is something very beautiful and desirable if it is taken in the sense that one should live free of passions arising in opposition to reason and confusing the spirit; but not even in this sense is it granted to earthly life. But if apatheia is taken to mean that a passion cannot even approach the spirit, this is the merest stupidity, is worse than all frailties taken together. In the thirteenth century Thomas Aquinas made such a fine distinction that it is still worthy of consideration in our day. "*Ex passione* agere diminuit et laudem et vituperium, sed *cum passione* agere potest utrumque augere" (*De Ver.* 26:7 ad 1). "To act from passion diminishes both honor and reproach, but to act *with* passion can increase both." The basis for this thesis is found in his writing *De Malo,* 12:1: "Because the nature of man is constructed of soul and body, of spirit and sensuality, it belongs to the good of man to devote himself *utterly* to virtue, namely with spirit, sensuality, and body alike."[28] Here Thomas expresses exactly what we mean today by integration-coherence. It is a fact that this purifying combination of intense passion and spirit does exist. There is a reason-controlled yet powerful passion to know, to investigate, to create artistically; to experience great and deep love in friendship and marriage and also to be truly religiously alive; a passion that more and more overcomes the dangers of primitive, purely instinct-driven, and blindly destructive behavior.

When we spoke of fanatic excitement we called fanatic paralysis its counterform; now we must confront fanatic passion with its *counterform of "colorless" fanaticism.* There is the pale fanatic who externally shows no conspicuous peculiarities. He vegetates in an instinctual-indolent, gloomy-brooding sense-imprisoned self and yet may one day perhaps become the talk of the town through a shocking act of violence. We may think here of some insignificant fanatic family tyrant or of those quiet and shy, very introverted subaltern individuals who suddenly someday terrify their neighborhood with an outbreak of brutality. Here the above-mentioned emotional ambivalence of the schizoid pointed out by Kretschmer can become a key for understanding.

We often meet this kind of colorless fanaticism in those women who, according to Jung, belong to the introverted feeling type.[29] These are the very inaccessible, quiet persons who seem to live out their days disinter-

ested and indifferent, with little contact with their fellowmen and current events. They look almost childishly
banal and seem to be cool and distant, give the impression of being frigid, but this is only on the outside. In
their depth burns an intense passion; an ideal is secretly
guarded and before an altar a heroic and wearisome-
pleasant cult is celebrated. They infiltrate their surroundings with a suffocating sense of superiority and seem to
exercise a mysterious power. It is especially their own
children who feel this power as a domineering force, as
a dictatorship of the most skillful pampering, as a fanatic
terrorizing through love. But if one day this power finds
itself confronting the resistance of those it has spoiled
it uses unscrupulous, base, and even foul means in order
to maintain its position. Then fanatic traits come mag-
nificently to the fore: Obstinacy, taking sides, intrigues,
"no pain is spared, even virtues are abused in order to
play the trump card" (Jung), hateful outbreaks occur and
the whole quiet, pallid enchantment turns into an explo-
sive chain reaction; intolerance with its entire suite of
somber relatives celebrates its feast of black magic. We
meet this type often enough in everyday life. But whoever would prefer to meet him masterfully portrayed in
literature should read Gertrud von Le Fort's novel *Der
römische Brunnen*, in which the character of Edelgart
as a quiet, pallid, but typically hysterical fanatic plays
one of the principal parts, or one may take up Graham

Greene's play *The Living Room,* where Helen in her
religious ethical fanaticism born out of fear drives her
young niece to suicide.

3. FANATIC RAGE OF WILL

Fanatic rage of will is another form of fanatic intensity,
to be differentiated from the forms of excitement and of
passion. We borrow the expression rage of will from
Klages; it points up a strange combination of the function
of will intellectually directed and vital instinctuality.
Thus the layer-specificity of the third form of fanatic
intensity is clearly designated: intelligence and instinct,
with the absence of the middle layer, namely of the
psychic, the empathetic, and the feelings.

Once more, however, we must come back to Wellek's
opinion that "fanaticism, because of its blindness on the
one hand and because of its rigor and coldness on the
other, is really more instinctual and instinct-determined
than is befitting the higher attitude of the will and has
nothing at all in common with the will that plans ahead
and insightful stability of will." In our opinion Wellek
here restricts the phenomenon of fanaticism too much
to certain forms of fanatic behavior and fails to see that
there are *other* forms of fanaticism which, despite the
restriction of the field of vision and the rigor and coldness, nevertheless have simultaneously working in them
a significant *recognition* and a deep, true *conviction*—for
instance, of a religious, social, scientific, or artistic kind.

Who would consider the fanaticism of Savonarola, Calvin, Lenin, or Stalin as merely instinct-determined? About the small and stocky Lenin with his satirical and scornful features we read: "He never appealed to the emotions and imagination but rather always to the will and determination; his speaking struggled with the listener, forced him to decision and left him no choice."[30]

The doctrine of psychic energy makes it clear that the energy of repressed psychic powers can intensify even to the point of absurdity the single power which is given admittance; this is why we speak about *rage of will,* in order to emphasize the intensification and constricting of the will's function. Yet this must not prevent us from seeing in some cases that the will is actually the *carrying* power of fanatic intensity. In this we feel in agreement with the conception of Klages, who speaks of the intensive hunger of the will which "demands satisfaction in the framework of the intellectual and especially in ethical relationships," and he adds: "Let us not fail to mention that the rage of will can also turn inward and thus cause abstinence-*fanaticism,* pleasure in self-martyrdom, and fakirism."[31] In this connection Klages refers mainly to the ethical rigorists and calls upon the well-known categorical imperative of Kant.

Ernst Kretschmer also implies an *intellectually* rooted fanaticism when he establishes his "schizothymic triad"— idealism, fanaticism, despotism—which he finds in Calvin, Robespierre, Savonarola, and Frederick the Great:[32]

Robespierre is not the bloodhound he is often pictured to
be but a "timid, gentle sentimentalist—a pale virtuous
ghost, a monstrous kind of schoolmaster without any
taste for monstrosity. He is well up in the literature of
the *contrat social,* his favourite reading, and with
pedantic exactitude he translates it into reality. He has
no idea what he is perpetrating. He goes on lopping away
with righteous integrity. He has no idea of anything
but—virtue and the ideal. He has no idea—that he is
hurting anyone. And meanwhile he writes poems like
Höolderlin, and is bathed in tears of emotion when he
speaks. . . . a virtuous murderer, an inhuman product
of humanity, 'A fanatic of cold reflexion gone mad.' "[33]
At another place Kretschmer says: "The instinct of cold,
bloody cruelty within the great heroes of world history
hardly appears with more clarity than in the founders of
virtuous nations. The most pure and abstract morality
of duty, the highest ethical idealism are the guiding aims
of despots like Robespierre. Why do they look so sullen
and gloomy? Why do they always have the hangman by
their side? They are the great men who have made
beheading a system; they have slaughtered hecatombs
of people in the prime of life on the altar of virtue,
have sent others into exile, coerced and tortured men
as though they were criminals—all in the name of
the good."[34]

Of course, Kretschmer was not alone in discovering
this fact. The saying "fiat justitia—pereat mundus" ade-

quately indicates that this type has always been known: the ethical and social rigorist who out of highest spiritual motives and resorting to his willpower has become the inexorably hard, cold, and cruel fanatic. It is by no means a contradiction when, in meeting resistance, the higher functions retreat more and more and gradually or suddenly give way to violent, instinctual impulses: The spiritual powers of the will are still at work and cannot be isolated from the total behavior of this type. Such a separation of will and instinct from the deliberations of reason becomes very clear in the case of Savonarola. Sementovsky, who sees Savonarola in a favorable light, says: "In that decisive moment of his life [alluding to Savonarola's reaction to his excommunication, 1497] indeed a change seemed to have taken place within him. It was as if he had suddenly moved away from rational considerations ordinarily so characteristic of him and succumbed to a kind of blind confidence in the power of his willing and his working."[35] This expresses very well the fusion of will and instinct and says precisely what we mean when we speak of "rage of will."

The *concrete manifestation* of this rage of will has already been shown in part in our discussion of its layer-specificity. We need merely to summarize it more concisely. The first trait we see is a *will for action* both hard and cold. These fanatics have a clearly outlined goal which must be reached under any circumstances and with ultimate effort. Their will for action is so strong that it can make them forget all other human needs. "They allow themselves no rest, they have no time to be tired, sacrifice every pleasure, recreation, their Sunday rest and strive to make all others do the same. There is something tormenting in their sense of duty, which can become a severe vexation for themselves, their family, and their place of work. All this does not spring from an exuberant pleasure in energy and work which has no limits, as in many hypomanics, but apparently from the most abstract idealism, from an a priori Kantian principle of duty."[36]

Such a will for action presupposes an almost mono-manic conviction and infusion of an ideal. It is as though this will-fanatic at any time and any place sees only *one thing*. The farsightedness for this one thing, how-ever, causes a shortsightedness and loss of insight for everything else. The overfocusing on a single point is simultaneously an underfocusing on the entire remainder of the field of vision. This is the only explanation for the Spartan rigor and the cutting coldness of these indi-viduals toward themselves and their entire environment. It is the cold ardor for the "monon" that dominates this type of fanatic and forces him forward, without tender-ness, without humor, without conciliation. For the schizo-thymic there is no "as-well-as" but only the inflexible, brutal "either-or." To resistance he responds with a "now all the more."

Such an attitude automatically abolishes any value-

consideration or questioning of means. An amoral unscrupulousness breaks through, escaping the notice of
the fanatic. "You are much too considerate in your
responses. Let me write a bit, then they will have an
answer that will make their ears ring and make it dawn
upon them," shouts the mystic-minded Savonarola on
March 1, 1498, from the pulpit of the cathedral of
Florence.[37] But he was seized by rage of will even before
this year of his burning; already in 1495 at least three
times, on three successive Sundays of October, he
thundered from the pulpit against Pietro de Medici:
"Cut off his head!"[38] Recall the raving Calvin when he
demanded that the judges "execute still many more
magicians,"[39] and how he indirectly denounced Michael
Servetus to the Inquisition, his own worst enemies.
Likewise Thomas Müntzer, the "rebel in Christ," had his
dark hour when "the revolutionary urge made him
demand the destruction of the 'godless' by force." He
wished to save "no one on this earth who resists the
word of God." He saw himself as the "destroyer of the
unbelievers and the one to whom God had entrusted the
'sword of Gideon.' "[40] Centuries later, in a completely
different world situation and with no religious idea of
being a chosen one but filled with the proletarian pathos
of a social revolutionary, the behavior of Lenin was
much the same. One could notice in Lenin "from the
very beginning a deep and inextinguishable *hatred* which
was aimed at the bourgeois like a clenched fist; in the

course of the years even his face seemed to have changed because of this fury." In the most difficult moments in his fight for power Lenin often repeated the statement he expressed on the eve of the October Revolution: "The good words are no praise for us. We rejoice only in the hateful cry of rage." This we know from Sinoviev, his close companion in battle, and he adds: "In it Lenin is completely revealed."[41]

Will for action, monomania, unscrupulousness, and hatred of enemies are the traits that characterize the fanatic of rage of will. Yet it would be incorrect to limit this form of fanatic intensity to only the great fanatics and the fanatic geniuses. There is also their pocket edition which we meet much more often. Think of those narrow-minded, atrophied pedants who suddenly see red when their life ideal is ignored. There are seemingly harmless stereotypes of a fanatic bureaucracy whose holy place is their office and whose sacred scriptures are printed forms; ordinarily they are somewhat ridiculous and pitiful figures who have, however, built an altar to their fanatic ideal, and they make themselves the high priests of a ritual which they celebrate unceasingly with precise monotony. What did Nietzsche say? "Fanaticism is the only strength of will which even the weak can achieve." But the tenacity and obduracy of these individuals, their touchiness, their hatred of everything out of the way, extraordinary, free, and independent is by no means less fanatically inspired than that of their great brother geniuses. Of course, this pocket edition of will-raging fanatics lacks the hot fire and the searing power of a truly high ideal, and so they become shabby, insignificant, and finally even ridiculous whenever they swell up into angry howlers or excited defenders of decency and decorum. They are a counterform of the significant, will-raging fanatic who electrifies, incites, and fanaticizes the masses.

For a clear understanding of fanaticism it is important to determine which of these three forms of fanatic intensity predominates in the concrete individual case. At times it is quite difficult to clearly differentiate and in some instances it may also be a matter of a slight shifting of accents where excitement, passion, and rage of will are tightly interwoven. Yet this must not keep us from recognizing the differences. Only in this way can the contradictions which we met in regard to the concrete manifestation of and the insight into fanaticism be gradually resolved.

If we are to make any preventive or even therapeutic headway into fanaticism it is again important that we differentiate these forms. Since excitement is strongly rooted in the psycho-physical organism as a unit, it is heavily dependent on the organic condition and can also be partly influenced by it. The unbounded, instinctive, and affect-conditioned passion, however, must generally be traced back to repression and damming up of the instincts and therefore needs the depth-psychological approach. Finally, rage of will points more strongly to spiritual energies and to value-experience as the motivating origin of the fanatic and instinctive will. Therefore the recognition and discussion of the spiritual problem should not be neglected.

III. THE VITAL-PSYCHIC BACKGROUNDS OF FANATIC INTENSITY

Why and for what purpose does man burn up so much energy through his instincts, his affects, and his will? Is he aware of certain motives or is he perhaps only the passive victim of unconscious energy processes? With this question we formulate the problem of the background of fanatic intensity. We use the term "background" in order to avoid the word "cause," since a merely causalistic thinking cannot grasp and adequately understand the psychic processes. Whether this background is in the last analysis a matter of the psychic structure, that is, a psychic constitution which gives rise to the disposition and is one of the causes of the states of wild excitement, burning passion, and cramped tightening of the will, or whether it is a more or less deeply rooted yet acquired attitude of experience at work behind the fanatic intensities must now be discussed. Our arguments should lead to the conclusion that in regard to this question an either-or viewpoint seems impossible and that the genesis of fanatic intensity involves the inter-

Fanaticism as a Problem of Intensity   49

action of all the various components, disposition, environmental experience, and even free self-determination.

1. INTENSITY AS SPONTANEOUS EXPRESSION OF VITALITY

As a first possible background of increased and seemingly fanatic intensity the spontaneous expression of elemental vitality should not be disregarded. There is the primordial vitality which always works with inordinate energy and carelessly and naturally spends itself in function-pleasure and exuberant feelings of energy.

Today we often meet hectically exaggerated and fanatically compulsive life expressions in the *urge for bodily movement* of the younger generation and at times even of the older as well. We are all acquainted with the *plaisir de mouvement* that needs to whirl in a dance and today tends toward rock 'n' roll and calypso and which at other times can also produce a riotous movement-storm—not necessarily always involving the smashing of tables and chairs by adolescent hoodlums. Sometimes this body-movement mania seeks to experience and prove itself in a pathological urge to set new records or in inciting the environment. Always the ultimate effort is made, to the point of exhaustion. These individuals seem incapable of acting differently. They yield semiconsciously to the movement-storm and are then completely seized and swept along by it.

We meet a similar phenomenon also in the *psychic-*

intellectual realm. We find here the same excessive function-pleasure in endless discussions and controversies, in
furious debates which at times look like playacting to the
outsider but for the participants are a psychic necessity.
The experience of one's own primordial intellectual vitality is not only extremely exciting but can also be instinctually, passionately, and inordinately enjoyable, so that
one will even deliberately repeat it again and again in
in order to enjoy it with ever-increasing intensity. Out of
exuberance and complete possession of all energies this
type seeks to devote himself to absolutely intellectual
space trips to the steepest climbs, the most daring curves,
and the wildest descents of intellectual problems and
pleasure in experiments, and he hereby reaches the verge
of intolerant fanaticism in the intoxicating experience of
his vitality. It is this pleasure-accented awareness that is
essential here. Dostoevski has portrayed with unparal-
leled mastery this at once pleasurable and self-tortured
search into spiritual labyrinths and has endowed his characters with a portion of fanaticism reaching the point of
the fanatic nihilism of Stavrogin, Raskolnikov, or Ivan.
Only the magic of extremes can incite in these individuals
the most hidden yet the most characteristic possibilities
and allure them into adventurous deeds.

Thus intensity based on spontaneous primitive vitality
need not always be connected with a simplification of
reality or even a disturbance of the reality-function,
despite the fact that this might appear necessary to pro-

duce such intensity. Even though we can ordinarily assume a certain loss of reality in the individual case, it can also be that only the most exhaustive expenditure of energy can fully cope with reality, correspond with it, grasp it, form and completely experience it. From this viewpoint an extreme "existentialistic" life attitude is somehow understandable.

Many adolescents need the boiling point of excitement: "Youth must have convulsions in its veins and foam on its lips," says a German proverb, and the Frenchman knows *la loi de la frénésie.* Those who say with Robert de Montesquiou: "Il n'y a de supportable que les choses extrêmes,"[42] are not the worst ones. Even in the religious realm we find the generally unconscious *goût de l'excessif* with aberrrations containing all forms of eccentricity, hysteria, and—fanaticism.

Not only the young but also people in general periodically manifest the need of experiencing the highest degrees of intensity and excess. After the torpor of everyday life people wish to experience a more passionate life: Mardi Gras, New Year festivities, harvest celebrations, and wedding-eve parties are then relatively harmless escape valves of such needs. People living in warmer climates need stronger things: bullfights, cockfights or even temple orgies allowing freedom from all restraints. Vitality in itself is experienced as *fanum.*

Therefore it is not surprising that serious investigators, such as Horstmann, seem to observe in most forms of

intense fanaticism a concommitant sexual undertone.[43]
The integration-coherence almost seems to demand such
a participation of the sexual apparatus. We know that
there are many cases in which what is sought is not so
much the satisfaction of instinct as rather instinct excitement; what is sought is a storm of excitement and the
highest degree of excitement is experienced as a pleasure-
goal. When the flagellants traveled in bands throughout
Europe this spectacle alone may have been for many the
stimulation of hidden and dammed-up instinctual intensities. From this point it is but step to sadistic-masochistic
actions.

Here we meet not the rigidity, the masking, the psychic
blocking, the congelation and petrifaction but rather an
overheating and overdrive of psycho-physical intensity by
which an individual not only becomes aware of his vitality
but also instigates, fascinates, and fanaticizes others to
such intensity. It is the same fanaticism of vitality and of
ecstatic expressions which manifested itself in earlier
millenia and in more archaic cultures in the form of
fertility cults, trance states, and dance orgies. When today
similar eruptions of primitive vitality with fanatic traits
are experienced, this phenomenon can perhaps only be
seen as a "countercourse," in that in our highly technological modern culture many needed expressions of primitive life are too much dammed up and one day break
through with primordial force. The danger of hysteria is
obvious in such a situation; we will deal with it later in

our treatment of delusional and compulsive ideas. Yet not only in hysterics but also in manic types spontaneous vitality can be observed as a background for fanatic behavior, in the manic and euphoric states intensity tumbles over itself. In the adolescent puritan and also when dealing with mass fanaticism, primitive vitality and the need for paroxysms must be taken into consideration as a possible background or component of fanaticism. It is quite possible that here the countenance of this fanaticism-gestalt can have hard and inexorable features, since the strong expression of vitality is bound to meet resistance which can be overcome only with a certain violence. Beyond this, however, it is characteristic that such fanaticism often cannot conceal a certain distortion into the grotesque, puerile, and even infantile.

Naturally, such elemental vitality is in most cases determined by the psycho-physical condition as a whole. By this we mean not only the endocrine processes but also the general chemico-physical changes of the plasm of the nerve cells, in connection, for instance, with lack of oxygen; there are also electrical phenomena which in turn can be created by climatic influences (atmospheric pressure, etc.) or by radioactivity.[44] It seems odd that the diagnosis of our above-mentioned six cases of eccentric fanatics at the clinic of Breslau mentions headaches in every case. Precise measurements of blood pressure and electroencephalograms could perhaps show pertinent parallel phenomena of a somatic kind.

Such deliberations should not lead us to the overhasty conclusion that all expressions of intensity or at least those of the motor system are due to somatic causes. The enthusiasm for an idea, whether religious, social, or political, whether expressed in ecstatic eruptions or even in fits of raving madness cannot be "explained" merely as a function of the blood pressure or of the glands, and so forth. Conversely, it would also be incorrect to see only psychic causes, for instance, compensatory needs, as source of the highest degrees of intensity. Such intensity is caused rather by a very complicated interplay of several somatic and psychic processes. According to recent investigations it seems almost certain that music can have a strong effect on metabolism and blood circulation; it can affect the blood pressure in such a way as to stimulate psychic activity or decrease manic hyperactivity. National anthems can stir emotional patriotism. We may here call to mind the effect of the *Horst Wessel* song of the National Socialists, the *Giovinezza* of the Fascists, the *Marseillaise,* and others. According to Pontvik there is evidence of "vital connection between blood pressure and patriotism"; this also represents a valuable contribution to the analysis of mass psychology.[45] Yet it would be wrong to distort such "vital connections" into a monistic theory of physiologic-vitalistic or spiritualistic tendency.

If we are willing to see the phenomenon of fanaticism on a broad base and not limit it to a single type of fanaticism we must take into consideration this background of primitive vitality and of an unbroken life tonus.

2. INTENSITY AS COMPENSATION

The astonishingly diverse and often careless *use of the concept of compensation* in depth psychology has been thoroughly discussed in David Hart's *Der tiefenpsychologische Begriff der Kompensation,* and now there is no excuse for a lack of awareness in the use of this concept. Yet, even according to Hart the formula which "can explain the essence of compensation" is "surprisingly simple and self-evident": compensation is "a reaction to a defect which tries to nullify the defect. When, despite this, the defect remains, then compensation also remains and a false equilibrium (overcompensation) is established. But when compensation nullifies the defect, then compensation, too, disappears."[46]

The fact of compensatory processes in both the biological and psychic realms of life must be seen and recognized as a universal basic tendency of all organisms and thus has the character of an elemental mechanism. Yet it must likewise be acknowledged that in the psychic life of the adult the unconscious self-healing tendencies and immanent regulating powers can be combined with a conscious control-authority of the ego or the self which can influence both a true and a false correction of the defect and thus contribute to a successful or unsuccessful compensation.

When we consider fanatic intensity of behavior to be
in some cases a compensation, or a conscious or unconscious attempt to solve a problem, we face here an important question: In what types of fanatics do we clearly
meet a compensation background of fanatic intensity
—that is, what defects are intended to be compensated
for consciously or unconsciously through intensity, and
what are the psychic consequences of the compensation intensity?

Even though the strongly value-conscious fanatics
and the fanatic geniuses can, to some extent, be rightly
understood only in a much more significant context
(about which we shall speak in the following chapter),
nevertheless the possibility of a compensatory function
of intensity as a "background" of their fanatic excitement, passion, and furious rage of will cannot be ex-
cluded. Obviously the defect intended to be balanced out
in such fanatics is of a special kind. It may be a repeatedly arising but also repeatedly and impatiently repressed
doubt in the value which the fanatic defends, a doubt
which he attempts to numb and hold down through
double and triple intensity of his involvement. C. G. Jung,
taking the viewpoint of the psychology of the unconscious, sees fanaticism as the "brother of doubt," as an
overcompensated inner doubt.[47] The more alarming the
doubt, the more often it makes itself heard, the more
compulsively it is repressed, and the more violent can
become the affirmations and professions of the value and,

above all, the more intense will be the defense against all attacks from the outside since these activate the inner doubt. This interpretation does not greatly differ from that maintained by Pfahler, according to which in certain types it is simply the resistance from the outside, the compulsion to prevail against a hostile environment, which requires fanatic intensity as resultant attribute. Frequently the continuous external resistance also awakens inner doubts about one's own viewpoint; one does not wish to admit this, and thus there are two "resistances," one from the outside and one from the inside, which cause the vehement eruption of intensity. (As is well-known, "resistance" in the psychoanalytic sense increases, the closer analysis approaches the true source of conflict, the neuroticizing complex.)

We see the effects of the combination of external resistances and inner doubts very clearly in a sermon of Savonarola two months before he was burned at the stake. Here he himself demurs: "Frate, you undermine the power of the Church. . . . O Frate, one must not defy the power of the Church. . . . Do not all the laws of the Church come from Christ? . . . Frate, you are in great danger. . . . What are you going to say now, Frate? What must you do? . . . Frate, how will your sensory part react to this?"

This was his last sermon in San Marco. One cannot read it without being deeply moved. For here it is no longer a matter of brilliant rhetoric or of scholastic method; here one senses how a great and noble man, for what he calls his ideal, is in combat with the world that more and more threateningly turns against him: as the noose grows tighter and tighter around his neck he can no longer suppress his doubts, and he voices them in the form of questions put to himself in person. Of course, it is also in this very situation that the inner compulsion begins to confirm itself through exaggeration and hectic intensity when he apostrophises: "Take vengeance, O Lord, for it has become unbearable down here. . . . When I lie then Christ lies, too." Finally he identifies with Christ: "Listen, thus speaks the Lord: You ask me to forego the sermon; I say to you, it is me whom you ask, not the Frate, for it is I who preach, not the Frate."[48]

It is the resistance of real or imagined enemies which also drives Nietzsche into ecstatic states of excitement. He had a very good insight into the mechanism of compensation and condemned "those men who have moments of sublime ecstasy, and who, on ordinary occasions, on account of the contrast and the excessive wearing away of their nervous forces, usually feel miserable and desolate," and who therefore "think of their environment, the age in which they live, and the whole world in which they have their being, with feelings of vindictiveness" (*The Dawn of Day,* aph. 50). Nevertheless, how many calories does he himself burn up for his own states of Dionysian ecstasy: "My enemies too are part of my bliss. And when I want to mount my wildest horse, it is always my spear that helps me up best . . . the spear that

I hurl against my enemies. How grateful I am to my enemies that I may finally hurl it! The tension of my cloud was too great: between the laughter of lightning bolts I want to throw showers of hail into the depths. . . . But let my enemies believe that *the evil one* rages over their heads" (*Zarathustra,* Part II, "The Child with the Mirror").

Here Nietzsche speaks with his "enemies," perhaps also with those within himself. Whenever he thinks of them an avalanche starts to move. All his inner doubts are projected onto an imaginary enemy and are silenced by the intensity of his Dionysian utterances.

It should be no surprise that the lesser geniuses, those who are less value-conscious, try to make up for some defect through fanatic intensity. They attempt to hide and compensate for their lack of experiential capacity, value-formation, lack of talent and of work-potentiality. While it is true that the absence of a burning idea and of true value fulfillment can lead to inner emptiness, narrow-mindedness and a gradual fade-out, it can also mislead one into the simulation of vitality. Through more intense means of expression and the highest degrees of excitement one at times puts on a show of passion on the stage of one's own psyche, thus intending to give a sense of value-experience and value-creation. Intensities are then produced and fanatically held onto, since only in this way can the semblance of having values be maintained. Affects have to be "borrowed."

Even authors who are not depth psychologists stress

compensation as a possible background of fanatic intensity. In 1941 Alfred Vierkandt in a rather simplified way
investigated the backgrounds of fanaticism in the Middle
Ages, which, according to his opinion, led to the Cru-
sades and later on to the Inquisition. He sees such backgrounds especially in the uprooting of medieval man,
caused in part by the "sudden rise of urbanization" (the
quick transition of great populations from a rural style
of life into the narrowness of small streets) and also in
part in the fact that "Christianity now truly gets a foot-
hold in the interior of man, while heretofore the pagan
spirit with its joy in total living had still been preserved."
"On two sides men were torn out of their rooted being
and expected to live a new style of life without the possibility of developing it in undisturbed purity in the first
generations: that is, there was a kind of uprootedness,
insecurity, and debility, and hereby also a certain agitation and inner unrest with tendencies toward depression,
fear, and anxiety. Out of this anxiety, in combination
with the debility of the psychic condition, originate the
well-known frequent and sudden changes from the
worldly to the spiritual (and also vice versa), the con-
versions and the renunciations. Thus medieval and late
medieval man dashes from violence into contrition, from
tears back into violence, from frenzied worldly activity
into fierce ascesis."[49]

Vierkandt also points out that in such circumstances
the scapegoat had to be found: the pagans, Jews, and the

heretics. Despite the obvious one-sidedness of this view, which fails to see several other backgrounds of the historical facts alluded to, Vierkandt's reference to the compensatory background is quite illuminating and very valuable for a legitimate psychological view of historical events and especially their fanatic character.

One may be tempted to see the uprooting of many people today and their overcompensation through fanatic intensities as a parallel situation, but, here, uprooting as due to the loss of an ultimate and absolute meaningfulness of existence and to being forced to adjust in the atomic era to a modern, technological style of life! Stertz too believes that the cause of an increased affectivity among eccentric fanatics is to be seen above all in a "disharmony and a lack of counterbalance of the psychic properties."[50] Miller de la Fuente goes even further. He sees in the unrestraint of the fanatic a symptom of inferiority, which manifests itself especially "as a lack of elasticity and hence as the incapability of entering into the world of thought or even the manner of thinking of one who thinks differently."[51] Likewise, Kujath stresses the point that the complete identification of the ego with the idea-system (hence the passionate excitement, and so forth) is a "way out of an inner disharmony and of the inflexibility of one's own nature."[52]

Fanatic intensity as compensation for a deficiency is a frequent phenomenon. The ill-prepared speaker who cannot speak and convince out of an inner value-experience depends on the power of impassioned pathos and feverishly works himself into dangerous pathways of thinking but above all into a fortissimo of emotions, not only convinced that they have always been effective but at the moment believing in them himself. His volcanic eruption has a sweeping, igniting, fanaticizing effect —even on himself.

Of course, the most common example of the need for compensation will always be that on the plane of simple vitality itself. The decline of biological potency, of life energy misleads many, especially today, into addictions which are supposed to create temporary peak intensities of experience or creativity. Alcohol, nicotine, amphetamine, drugs, opiates are supposed to stimulate. Rhythmic movements, drumbeats, dancing, monotonous songs, glaring colors are supposed to bring the sensory apparatus, and through it the psychic organism, into an elevated, active mood and at times even into a hectic ecstasy in which man feels his vitality even though his spontaneous vitality has already diminished or been used up. Thus fanaticism can be seen as a form of *addiction.* As we know, fanatic intensity is capable of creating the sweet venom of euphoric states and hence can be the desired compensation for defects, inferiorities, and guilt feelings.

It is clear that a compensation dynamics limited to intensity-increase is not very deep and cannot satisfy the real value needs of the psyche. Increase of intensity based on compensation dynamics can merely activate the impulses and make one work harder; it stimulates one to work but does not give the interiority which determines *what* is really done. Creative values never owe their existence merely to a compensation impulse caused by an inferiority complex. There is even danger that such compensating intensity reduces all the more the reality function and thus causes the intensity fanatic to make the fatal mistake of bypassing reality and the real world of values.

The consequences of this compensation dynamics are obvious. Depressive moods raise their voice ever more strongly and in their wake the frightening life anxiety grows. This anxiety, if not resolved from a conscious value viewpoint, can only be pacified and anesthetized by an even more feverish compensation intensity. The vicious circle is now closed. The only thing still to be said is simply this: that there is no object which cannot serve as a means of momentary simulation of an overpowering sense of life. One can just as easily shift from sports fanaticism to work fanaticism, from the paroxysm of the dance to the burning fires of religious activity, from the demon of knowledge to the fever of justice (e.g., Gregers in Ibsen's *The Wild Duck*). As psychological function there is no difference. Intensity in these instances is like a monsoon blowing over the dryness of burned-up soil. "Il n'ya de supportable que les choses extrêmes." The disgust for the ordinary and the *horror vacui* keeps the whirlwind in motion. The deep psychic misery of these intensity fanatics should now be quite clear. Behind the fanatic intoxication an inner cry of distress must be heard.

The problem that now arises is that of the relationship between fanaticism and inauthenticity. Is not fanaticism as compensation always a conscious, half-conscious, or unconscious inauthenticity caused by the lack of vital or psychic-spiritual powers and hence grounded in hysteric lability? We will discuss this question when we deal with the pathological components of fanaticism.

3. INTENSITY AS ABSOLUTIZING DRIVE

Neither spontaneous vitality nor a compensation dynamics are sufficient to explain in all cases the development of extreme fanatic intensity, of the sweeping rebellion of the entire psychosomatic potential, and so we must ask whether perhaps there are still other backgrounds to be taken into consideration in certain cases. The term *fanum* means sacred place and in antiquity the fanatic was considered to be one possessed by God, one put into raging enthusiasm by a deity—that is, an individual who could no longer be encompassed within the categories of natural understanding. No matter how reserved our general attitude toward preternatural interpretations may be, we have no right to simply throw aside age-old ways of explanation without further ado. Although we may be unwilling to acknowledge even for the most exceptional cases a direct intervention of the

transcendent God as background for a clear state of
fanatic trance, we must nevertheless take into consideration the possibility that such intensity-phenomena may
be the "God within us"[53] and that the natural capacity
of the psyche, which along with Caruso we call "absolutizing drive," may be at work and a natural gravitation
of the psychic center may hereby be seeking a perfect
expression of that which is always necessarily imperfect.
When we meet ecstasy at its wildest and intensity reaches
ecstatic dimensions, it may perhaps sometimes be a matter of something ultimate and supreme where man wants
to touch the absolute. Intensity can then become the
symbol-bearer of the absolutizing drive—and can even
become an *absolutum* itself.

To say that intensity is a spontaneous eruption of
vitality is not a satisfactory explanation, especially in
regard to fanatic geniuses, to men of science, artists,
mystics, politicians, and social reformers. Hardly ever
do we find historically important and classic fanatics
among the extremely healthy or even the cyclothymic
manics but mostly in the schizothymic area. They are
often frail and small in stature, leptosome, asthenic,
gaunt cerebrotonics, pallid with unhealthy yellow pig-
mentation, with the typical angular profile described by
Kretschmer; they are constantly irritated and nervous
and drive both themselves and others. Think of Savonarola and his speech difficulties, of Calvin's feminine
sensibility,[54] of Robespierre, who drank his glass of milk

every morning and the rest of the time lived a more ascetic life than a monk, "with a haggard face, bilious complexion and dried-up manners . . . his hands, shoulders and eyelids affected at times by convulsive twitching," or we may look at the portrait of his disciple Saint Just with his soft feminine face and ivory white forehead as he cooly and impassionately, unyieldingly and rigidly pleads with perfect logic for the death of the king. In all these fanatics the psychic background of their rage, their unrestrained fury, and their unscrupulous cruelty is not spontaneous vitality, for this vitality was not theirs to have.

But neither can the background of a half-conscious or unconscious compensation dynamics completely explain the inexorable, systematically ultra-hard attitude of these characters, for, as we know, there are often men of highest value-experience who have no need to compensate their lack of talent or of value-fulfillment with external intensity. Even though vital and psychic disharmony may lead them to temporary compensatory behavior, we would do them no justice if we see their fanatic intensity merely as adjustment or ersatz. To reduce in all cases the extremes of psychic intensity to "nothing but compensation" is unsatisfactory. The drive to exceed all established limits, the knocking on all walls, the shaking of all gates at times points to a power arising from the depths and seeking the *very ultimate*.

Dostoevski, in his *Notes from Underground,* investigated this passionate, seemingly senseless monster and

in some of his characters (Ivan in *The Brothers Karamazov*) its most hidden stirrings. These individuals cannot
stop it, they are truly obsessed by a mania for the "completely other," the eternal, the everlasting. They are con-
sumed by a *recherche de l'absolu* that drives them into
further unrest. We should perhaps call to mind here the
great movement which in the twelfth century extended
into great parts of the West: the Cathari or Albigenses.
They attempted to realize a perfection which left all
other Christian standards far behind. They represented
a claim of religious totality which no longer had any eye
for the worldly. Their will for the absolute had become
such an all-consuming fire that they not only rejected
everything material, all eating of meat, every joy, even
marriage, but went so far as to experience the "endura,"
the voluntary death by starvation as the high point of
the fight against evil.[55]

Yet it is not simply the by nature absolute, the transcendent God who is met in this intensive seeking but
rather something relative which, as transitory parable, as
copy of the original, manifests itself laden with value but
nevertheless in itself cannot give ultimate fulfillment. The
danger that such a relative value then becomes absolutized and that one, so to speak, "makes something a
God" is quite obvious. Jung, in his psychology of the
unconscious, has explicitly pointed out this quid pro quo.[56]

From this intensity which manifests itself as absolutizing drive it seems but a short step to the attitude which
experiences and also *seeks* to experience intensity as the

absolute itself. As we have already explained intensity
is a quantitative category which in its different forms and
degrees is in the service of other values, but especially
in the phenomenon of fanaticism we see the strange possibility of the quantitative category turning into a *qualita-
tive category*. Intensity itself can be experienced as value,
even as the supreme value. It is not only modern technology which shows us this possibility; long before the
power-driven motor, the symbol of our time, the simple
wheel was for millenia the symbol of eternal motion.
Heraclitus with his *panta rhei* had already moved fluctu-
ation, motion, and hereby intensity into the sphere of the
absolute: Intensity as infinite process. Intensity, the dynamic, becomes the *fanum*, the sacred sign of a higher
existence, of a value-filled existence. Did not Goethe, at
the end of his *Faust*, elevate intensity to the saving element of redemption? And does not Rilke say: "One must
only keep going"? The eternal unrest becomes a metaphysical power. Exuberance as such becomes a real power
of being and takes on the highest splendor.

We also encounter a *distortion* of this most sublime
development of intensity: Instead of "divine fury" (Plato),
instead of the existential unrest of the heart of Augustine
("Our heart will not rest until it rests in God"), the
spiral of endless anxieties, of psychic torment, of gnaw-
ing restlessness keeps constantly narrowing within man.
We recognize these constantly and unrelentingly tor-
mented individuals who are closed up in their anxiety
neurosis as though in an underground prison. Generally

they themselves are aware of the "unfoundedness" of these anxieties, but they are still unable to free themselves from their terrorizing power and tight grip. The intensity of anxiety increases and is experienced almost concretely as a suffocating force. Thus in these cases too it is not always merely the existential life anxiety as such (which, as we know, is part of human existence) but its suffocating intensity which is experienced as quasi-absolute.

Intensity in this ultimate extreme manifests itself as a purely subjective category, as an innermost fire which either draws everything into the light or sears and burns everything. Not infrequently such ultimate intensity is seen as the criterion of authentic experience. One admits authenticity only when he is on fire with the highest degree of intensity; only then does he believe in an inner purity and honesty of feeling, thinking, and acting. But the question now arises: What is normal intensity? How do we distinguish between spontaneous vitality and ersatz intensity, and at what point do we encounter intensity which is legitimately called *recherche de l'absolu?* Is not all enthusiasm and every ebullient expression already exaggerated, inadequate, and disproportionate to the narrow-minded know-it-all? The criterion cannot be found in intensity itself, but there must be a different approach for its discovery. In order that fanatic intensity be rightly understood still other measures must be taken. A different view of the whole idea of fanaticism is called for.

CHAPTER TWO

Fanaticism as a Problem of Value-Attitude

I. THE SELF-CONCEPT OF THE FANATIC

What strikes us first and foremost in regard to the fanatic is the intensity with which he fights for his cause. The cause itself, the idea, the value for which the fanatic so intensely battles seems to the outsider, and often even to psychological observation and opinion, to be of very secondary importance. At first glance this seems reasonable enough, for it is the very "going beyond," the ultra-dimensional in the fanatic's behavior—in other words, his intensity—which makes him conspicuous to his invirons. If all human experience and activity is to be understood as a subject-object relationship, then in the fanatic's case it is his autocratic, subjective way of defending an objective value which at first characterizes him as psychologically "interesting." Stertz says, "The content of fanatical idea-orientation is of subordinate importance in comparison with the form of the supporting frame of mind."[1] When psychiatry and psychotherapy speak of "overvalued" ideas and images they basically mean by this simply that in the individual case and in view of the concrete totality of the psychic household too much psychic energy and energetic intensity is given to a particular idea. In the individual case this judgment seems to be grounded in the obvious psychic disturbance which occurs in such a lopsided distribution of energy. For who can say how much "value," how much libido, what quantity of psychic energy can objectively and legitimately be expended on an idea or an imago? This would presuppose a universally recognized hierarchy of values.

Does this mean then that we should, in our investigations of fanaticism, disregard the significance of the idea, of the "value per se," considering it of less importance, or at best mention it at the margin as a secondary problem? Such an omission would in fact hinder any possibility of a psychic understanding of the fanatic. The objective value-relationship must be taken very much into consideration for a correct view of the fanatic, and this all the more since the fanatic himself ordinarily does not consider himself different from those around him because of the intensity of his behavior. What is more often in the foreground of his consciousness is the idea or value which he fights for or against. This *self-concept* of the fanatic should not be bypassed if we are to investigate fanaticism without prejudice. Thus we need a careful examination of the fanatic's *value-attitude,* and this will, in fact, illumine important and at times inadequately considered contexts.

In the first place the fanatic with his value-attitude simply shares the universal human need for a value-filled existence. The importance of a central idea, of a fulfilling value seems generally necessary for a meaningful existence. If we are to avoid from the very start the presupposition that behind every fanatic value-attitude there are only and exclusively pathological dispositions or psychic shiftings of pathological character, we must try to point out also the positive backgrounds of such an attitude.

Here unquestionably we touch on the natural value-need, which also in many types of fanatic value-attitudes plays a great role. Therefore we believe that the universal value-need and the innermost value-relationship of man must be considered as essential in any humanist psychology, since they cannot be replaced by purely energetic viewpoints or a mere description of behavior. The recognition and consideration of the psyche's orientation toward values is decisive for its understanding even when pathological symptoms are manifested. No psychological investigation can bypass the specific place of value without falsifying the human position. In this regard we demand for fanaticism only what we must demand for the understanding of most kinds of psychic behavior in a humanist psychology. In this context we may call to mind the valuable typology of Eduard Spranger, which gives interesting insights into man's specific value-areas.[2]

Even though the definition of "value per se" depends on the particular philosophy in question, the psychology of consciousness has long referred to value-discernment, value-experience, value-decision, and so forth, with the unexpressed presupposition that everyone knows what "value" is. A quite general definition of the term states, for instance, that value is "the being itself, inasmuch as, by virtue of its content, it signifies a perfection and thus induces striving,"[3] or, in other words, values are those determinants of an object which are decisive for its perfection or imperfection so that according to their presence or absence a value-judgment takes place. Value is experienced and striven for as an expansion of being, as an enrichment and enhancement of existence.

The depth psychology of C. G. Jung and, even more emphatically, the approaches of more recent depth psychology point out the need of considering the intended value in human behavior.[4] Jung emphasizes that the "complex," the conglomeration of psychic energies, must be seen not only as a danger but likewise as an opportunity, even as a necessary condition for every cultural achievement.[5] But it is formed around an "elemental core," around an "imago," an idea which is felt as value. In fact, Jung clearly advocates a hierarchy of values when he says, "I therefore consider it wiser to acknowledge the idea of God consciously; for, if we do not, something else is made God, usually something quite inappropriate and stupid such as only an 'enlightened' intellect could hatch forth."[6]

Thus it will be quite difficult to refuse value its deserved place within the subject-object relationship.

Fanaticism as a problem of value-attitude allows us to take a first look at various types of fanatic value-attitude. Subsequently we will have to consider more closely the psychic backgrounds of this attitude in these various types.

II. VARIOUS TYPES OF FANATIC VALUE-ATTITUDE

We will now proceed to differentiate three typical groups of fanatic value-attitude, and in doing so we are completely aware that it will be difficult at times to put the fanatic into a particular category or classify him as a pure type. All typologies have the same problem; nevertheless, scientific typologizing has heuristic and pragmatic value. In limiting our viewpoint to three groups of fanatic types we are not attempting to simplify the complexity of the specific and particular phenomena of fanaticism into a few categories or to give a relatively complete typology of fanaticism from the viewpoint of value-attitude. Our intention is simply to use the value-standpoint in order to see and understand the problem of fanaticism on a broader basis. A differentiation of types seems to be meaningful and worthwhile since it not only sharpens our eye for certain forms and forces us to a more precise observation of the individual case but it also expands our perception of the total phenomenon of fanaticism. The following three group-types of fanatics are met not only in everyday life but also in pertinent literature without any reference to principles of classification. From the viewpoint of value, fanatics can be classified into groups separating the fanatic with an external formalistic attitude toward value from one who maintains an inner relationship to the form or the content of the value.

1. TYPES OF FORMALISTIC VALUE-ATTITUDE

At the lowest level of value-attitude are the fanatics of an almost empty and purely external formalism. In these there is not only no true interior relationship to a concrete and definite value-content but they lack even the inner experience of the form in which this value is represented. We see only a bleak, naked, literally empty, formalistic, and, for the most part, externally forced value-attitude which at the moment is defended or attacked. Value in its proper meaning, as content, as "substance," falls into second place if it is not completely insignificant. Value as such is unimportant and can therefore undergo several variations in the course of one's life. Such changes of external value come from external causes, for instance "orders from above" or external circumstances that make an adjustment seem advantageous. In the foreground of the one so ordered is a completely impersonal attitude, and the order is carried out in practice from an inflexible, either-or standpoint as a rigid and stubborn insistence on all-or-nothing.

On the lower level these are the rabid, professional warrior-types, the tough get-the-job-done characters who look neither right nor left. Kogon describes the SS men as follows:

"Hitler's SS, almost without exception, are an example of the effectiveness of a psychological schema: A few sharply fixated, dogmatic, unresolved, simplified contents of consciousness form a hard crust of brain beneath which lurks a mob of emotion. They are impenetrable to true insights and ideals, they instinctively only seek ways out within the *prescribed explosion-channels.* All SS men known to me and my friends were barbarians in this sense, without any element of culture, that is, without any capability of forming spirit and instincts into a higher psychic unity. This judgment is valid for everyone in their ranks; without exception those who were really SS men and not incidentally thrown or forced into the SS and so never capable of identifying with the Black Shirts were savages whose psychological behavior always expressed itself as that of a type rather than that of an individual."[7]

"Thus everything perpetrated by the SS in the concentration camps, whether by an individual or by the gang, is psychologically no puzzle at all: it was the action of men already endowed with particular intellectual, emotional, and social prerequisites who were trained in this way and given such a task. They were trained to track down public enemies, to give the proper treatment to those who wronged the people, and to 'do away' with 'the enemies of the Führer'."[8]

Kogon's description is confirmed by a large number of statements made by the SS men themselves. For example, let us listen to what Adolf Eichmann, who was responsible for the transportation of the Jews to the annihilation camps, said before court:

"Captain, if at that time someone would have said to me: 'your father is a traitor,' that is, that my own father was a traitor and I should kill him I would have done it. I stubbornly obeyed my orders and found in them my fulfillment and my reassurance in the struggle of fate of the German people, as it was called and as we could not understand differently, no matter what order I may have been given."[9]

The role of value-content is scarcely more important in the similarly shallow, hollow, formalistic value-attitude of those *busybodies* and feverish *activists* who get involved in things, whether it be simply one predominant value, or several simultaneously, or one right after the other. For activists and busybodies the concrete value is only a very incidental object and is not experienced in its actuality and significance by the entire person. The activist can be concerned with the highest problems of mankind, with political, social, scientific, and religious goals and likewise with extremely banal everyday problems; he can fanatically throw himself into them with all his strength, as though it were a question of to be or not to be, but one is soon astonished to discover that he has once more changed his position and now defends the opposite viewpoint with the same hectic flurry. Value for him is a mere accretion and does not impose an inner obligation; the specific value is not formed into a specific way of experiencing and living: one activist propagates religion just as another represents his champagne company or sells soap. It need not be mentioned that among this type we obviously do not find fanatic geniuses or the great fanatics. But among the "little" fanatics the activist can occupy a prominent place. Their fanatic profile often shows very distinct instinctual and compulsive traits. We may call to mind here the enthusiasts and fanatic propagandists.

But even on the *higher, intellectual level* we meet this type of a merely external value-formalism. This is the person who indulges in endless hairsplitting and thought- and word-acrobatics, in a mere playing with empty, shallow words or phrases, a simple make-believe in which reckless and risky formulations and paradoxes are thrown like balls. We often find this type among the highly intelligent who quickly catch the weakness of every position and every intellectual statement and, in an impassively relativistic attitude, attack it or, for a change, once in a while defend it—"assimilate" would say too much. No real dialogue, no deep psychic "engagement" takes place. In fact, his own noncommittal attitude can be experienced as a new "value," which he may even fanatically advocate in contradiction to his otherwise skeptical attitude. The interior idling of his intellectual motor (the atrophy of the emotional life is here clearly recognizable) which without true depth of experience seizes upon values and words merely for the purpose of obdurate self-assertion, external show, and a situational "superiority" forces him at times to put on the face and gravity of a real and true value-experience. Often enough such an individual then tends to become more and more radical and hence more and more suspect. In such instances the most inordinate positions are always formulated, the "ultimate" is demanded, there is a display of extremes but extremes about which one rightly says "les extrêmes se touchent"; but give him a little time and the opposite position will be defended with equal passion and cold logic. It would be psychologically shortsighted to call such a process an "inner development." We want merely to point out here the possibility and the existence of this type.

In the political realm such fanatic intellectual humbugs are generally the "party-stallions," who use every

trick in the book in their pursuit of a cunning and reckless, high-flying ideology, which offers its rigid yet prolix
vocabulary of slogans for political purposes. We find an
especially interesting example of this type in the history
of the anarchic revolutions in Russia at the time of the
Czar Alexander II. At that time the Netchaev case created a great sensation, and Dostoevski used it as the
outline for his novel *The Possessed*.

Netchaev was an anarchist-nihilist who undoubtedly
deserves to be the subject of a detailed biography. Where
anarchism was concerned he was a fanatical idealist;
apart from this, his personal character was as base and
immoral as anything in criminal history. His intrigues
show him to have been as degraded as Lacenaire, and
he was as ruthless and brutal as any Nazi thug. Yet his
life shows an extraordinary, perverted heroism. There
is even a story that he helped to plan the assassination
of Alexander II while he was imprisoned in the Peter and
Paul Fortress (Russia's 'Devil's Island'), and that when
his associates asked whether they should concentrate
on rescuing him or on killing the Tsar, he answered
without hesitation 'Remove the oppressor.' The 'oppressor' was removed, and Netchaev died of scurvy in prison.

"Netchaev, the 'tiger cub,' was one of the world's
most remarkable deceivers; he tried to build up a vast
revolutionary movement solely on lies, bluff, and playacting. He deceived everybody (including the arch-
revolutionaries Bakunin and Herzen) and might easily,

with a little more luck, have intrigued his way to absolute dictatorship of Russia (which was obviously his ideal).

"The affair that provided the plot of *Devils* [*The Possessed*] led to Netchaev's downfall. In Moscow, posing as the representative of a certain 'European Revolutionary Alliance,' Netchaev organized small groups of students and disillusioned ex-Army officers into 'revolutionary committees.' A student named Ivanov was suspected of planning to betray them, and was murdered by Netchaev, with the complicity of the 'group.' The murder was soon discovered; arrests followed. Netchaev escaped to Switzerland, then to England, while the affair occupied the front pages of Russia's newspapers. Later, Netchaev, with misplaced confidence in the authorities' short memory, walked back into the lion's mouth, and ended in the Peter and Paul Fortress."[10]

A more harmless representative of this type is the notorious know-it-all who with his fast draw shoots down every opponent even if, in the heat of the moment, he constantly contradicts himself. Such a know-it-all can give the impression of being quite fanatic, but the value viewpoint which becomes visible is purely formalistic.

A certain type of yellow journalism which handles the *chronique scandaleuse* with well-trained moral indignation and great effectiveness often furthers such fanatics of the moment. When important issues are scarce, those of secondary importance are played up and the emotions of the masses are artificially stimulated. Important human and cultural values seem suddenly to be at stake but just as suddenly disappear again from the field of awareness, since this kind of journalism needs ever new scandals in order to stay alive. The producers of this type of journalism are not fanatics themselves but merely skillful dancers on every intellectual-philosophical or religious-moral tide who enjoy the incitement of fanatic flare-ups in the ordinarily indolent masses. They master the reckless jargon of a despirited consumer society, but they lack a true inner relationship to value and thus the basis for responsible journalism.

Hereby we do not wish to deny that there is also the type of great and true "dialectician" who painfully experiences the polarity of all relative being to its full extent and passionately represents this in magnificent paradoxes. Such problem-weighted dialecticians are distinguished from the aforementioned humbugs by an immeasurable inner world of values: Let us call to mind, for instance, Meister Eckhart, Blaise Pascal, or Goethe, men of a great and mature world view who, perhaps for this very reason, in their honesty felt it necessary to withdraw more and more into silence.[11]

It should be clear then that, with the exception of these last-mentioned great dialecticians, the types we have just been describing—despite their peculiar and unmistakable fanatic tendency and at times even their ineradicable bent for fanatic behavior—show that they do not represent fanaticism in its "high form." We put these types in the "low" forms of fanaticism since they are insignificant and inconsistent in their value-attitude. Thus relationship to value allows at least an external ranking. To what extent also the inner, subjectively psychic rank is lower than the two following groups will be clarified in our section about the psychic background of this specific value-attitude. It seems, moreover, that the minimal inward relationship to value often imprints on this type of fanatic a brutally rough, cynically unstable, even perfidious and base trait of character. The intellectual humbug himself does not always avoid this crudely primitive behavior in the corresponding situation.

2. TYPES OF FORMAL VALUE-ATTITUDE

The formal value-attitude in question here is not an external, incidental, imperated attitude toward some kind of value but an inner, psychically rooted attitude toward a very definite value in the concrete case. This value is the *form* in which an idea, an object, presents itself. Even though this form is combined with the content, or at least can be combined with it, it should not be confused with it. We are aware of the fact that we herewith touch on a very difficult and almost insoluble question. The relationship between content and form is very complex and therefore needs a fundamental, even though brief, clarification.

The form can fuse into such a unity with the content that it seems impossible to experience each separately.

In this instance we speak of the "inner form" which determines the configuration almost in the manner of an organic law of nature, as a directional law (entelechy). Scholasticism refers to the *forma substantialis* and distinguishes it from the *forma accidentalis*. We find this inner form most clearly in the configurations of nature. Goethe sees in it the "primitive phenomenon" that creates astonishment: "Nature is neither core nor shell, it is everything at once." Great works of art can also show this unity of form and content so perfectly and thus so inseparably that they appear perfect and lead from an aesthetic to a religious experience. Hölderlin felt that the true poem had this character: "If one day I succeed in the sacred which is my concern, the poem, welcome, then, oh silence of the world of shadows; for once I lived as the gods and no more is needed." The experience of an artistic inner form can also become an ersatz, as experienced by Gottfried Benn: "Only form is faith and deed." Finally we find also cultural and religious institutions, for instance, a several-centuries-old political institution or an ancient religious community which, almost like a being of nature, has an organically grown gestalt. (The Church is compared to a growing seed.)

Yet at times the form is merely a garment constantly changed and thus appearing as purely "external" form. Of course, we should take into account that even such an external form can not only be experienced as value but in certain instances and under certain aspects can be even more important than the content. We may call to mind here the art of costuming of some of the sculptures and paintings of the sixteenth century or the Cosmati works of the medieval churches of Rome and especially the figurations of the reproducing arts and of artistic handicraft: The form itself is the content. Nonetheless we must remain aware of the distinction.

There are both form-fanatics of the external form and those of the internal form. In the particular case the distinction is at times quite difficult. But it seems only right to classify the internal-form fanatic with those types who have an inner relationship to the value-content. At this point we will deal with the external-form fanatic.

The external-form fanatic experiences the masterful formal shaping as value in itself and as value supreme. We meet these form-fanatics in all areas of value, very often in the aesthetic-artistic realm but with equal radicalism in the ethical area (in a pharisaical defense of rigorous discipline) and at times also in the realm of law when the formal juridical viewpoint becomes a fetish. Finally we find it also in the religious realm, for example, in the form of an irritable, oversensitive insistence on the most minute ritual prescriptions or on their immediate "restoration" or change, even if circumstances make this impossible.

No small problem arises with this kind of attitude. Can the external form possibly be experienced as a value in itself, isolated from the specific content? Can certain forms—for example, those of human social life ("good manners," "refinement," "aristocratic behavior"), of public juridical life (prescriptions and regulations), or of creative art (the perfection of technique, supreme mastery of the language of form)—can any one of these, independent of its significance, represent a value in itself and even be experienced as supreme value?

The fact that these form-fanatics do exist, moreover that they defend their "value" with the intensity and violence of an actual obsession forces us to answer this question in the affirmative. We would fail to see the true facts if we should seek to point out the seeming contradiction that the "form"—which is always a "measure," a proportion—is thrown into the heat of the battle in such an immeasurably and formlessly radical way. The identification of form and measure, of form and proportion has existed in the history of art and culture only in certain epochs, whereas the archaic art of a beginning culture, for instance, ordinarily displays disproportionate and measureless structural forms in the service of religious ideas and since 1900 modern art has dedicated itself to entirely different form-experimentations.

By no means should the external-form fanatics be put on the same level psychologically with the formalistic fanatic types. In the external-form fanatic we find a true experience of form which in the specific case shows a clear individual gestalt and is generally rooted deep in the structure of the person. On the other hand it would be difficult to equate them psychologically with the inner-form fanatics of a high value content. The external-form fanatic seldom remains this for his whole life or even for an extended period of time. His drive for perfection forces him to thrust sooner or later toward the content of the idea—or else we may meet him sometime later as a negator of form or even as a destroyer of form; but even here this attitude can be of transitory character. Whereas in the formalistic fanatic the change of his external position is almost a natural part of his profile, the form-fanatic of the external form often undergoes a change of experience which occurs with a certain necessity, a necessity which can be effected innerpsychically, for instance, in the sense of the "regulating function of the opposites."

From the great group of form-fanatics we shall present only two types: the artistic form-virtuoso and the ethical perfectionist, since these two represent the type very convincingly and can be met relatively often.

The Form-fanatic in the Realm of Art—In the artistic realm it is chiefly the representational artists, virtuosos, actors, dancers, and ornamentalists who often strive with fanatic energy for the formal ideal of perfection. The representational virtuoso must strive for the immaculate form in a process of constant refinement. Precision and subtlety of expression are the determining and decisive elements of every convincing re-creation. As important and irreplaceable the experience of the idea and of the inner content may be, this very experience generally seems to come to the fore and to deepen only by way of the experience of the form and its authentic reproduction. The desire for a perfect external form-reproduction of a creative work of music through its masterful performance or for a perfect presentation of forms of a dance can lead to very rigid, stubborn, and even aggressive behavior.[12]

We may call to mind here the actions of certain conductors who "uncontrolledly"—or better: in unlimited perfectionism—shout at even first-class musicians and who make every rehearsal a "tensile test." Richard Wagner, at a rehearsal of *Parsifal,* in Bayreuth, sent a Gralsritter singer off the stage merely because he was smiling, with the remark: "Whoever laughs now cannot be a good person." Architecture, too, often paid a fanatic toll, in classicism and "purism," to the form-ideal. We find a clear overemphasis of form in the paintings of the ornamentalist—Beardsley, for instance—and, of course, in the unobjective, abstract painting of cubism, futurism, and surrealism. In these approaches the form-problems of proportion, parallelism, and color rhythm are necessarily predominant. The shaping of the form likewise occupies a supreme position in certain recent poetical works, for instance in the word-sound creations of the dadaism of a Hugo Ball, August Stramm, Kurt Schwitters, Rudolf Blümner, Richard Behrens, and so forth. We may recall Hugo Ball's "Programmatic Words" preceding a recitation in Zurich in 1916: "With this kind of sound-poem one should renounce lock, stock, and barrel a language that has been spoiled and made impossible by journalism. One should retreat into the innermost alchemy of the word and even abandon the word and thus preserve for poetry its ultimate and most sacred realm. One should refuse to compose second-hand poems, that is, to utilize words (not to speak of sentences) which are not newly invented for one's own purpose. . . ."[13]

We must point out here the *magic* of the form. Form can not only enthuse and move but can captivate, fascinate, and even numb so as to place man in a different psychic mood, in the beginning of a "state of trance" where he has a completely new kind of experience and senses within himself unimagined higher powers. Jagged rhythms, drawling chords, heavy, suggestive movements, inventive variations on a theme, and the sharpest contrasts strongly produce this magic effect, the relationship with a more beautiful and more powerful world. Thus it is the formal means of presentation and representation which, as we know, are put to use also in realms other than the arts and which are used very consciously and even with skillful calculation, for example, in political propaganda and in many other kinds of mass-influence.

Just how much fanatic traits can permeate the form-experience and even become dominant can be seen, for instance, in the "manifestos" of cubism, futurism, and surrealism proclaiming their system to the world as the only true one. They believe themselves the exclusive owners of the soul-saving art: "Standing at the top of the world we once more throw our challenge to the stars,"[14] the futurists declare. Derain, "with almost scientific rigor, pushes the form into pure culture,"[15] while Signac holds on to his substantiation of neo-impressionism "like a teaching of dogma."[16] At times Nolde covers up his sensitivity and shy reserve "with an almost fanatical spirit of aggression and the unconditional will to carry out what he has acknowledged as right."[17]

Also pertinent here are the heated arguments in some groups of artists where schisms, excommunications, and the most furious attacks are by no means the exception. Spiteful polemics, crude manners of expression, and calumniation of the opponent, who is called a "philistine," at best, and generally an "idiot," indicate that for the artists concerned the issue at hand is a matter of the very ultimate, of a *fanum* involving their whole existence: The beautiful is also the "sacred." While outsiders shrug their shoulders: "de gustibus non est disputandum," for these artists the ultimate and the supreme is at stake. The hope which the form-fanatic at times places in political movements, his readiness for battle for the most extreme tendencies—we may think here of the susceptibility of some great artists to communism[18]—and also the disappointment which he generally experiences after a short time prove how "seriously and sacredly" he takes it when he seeks to assist in the breakthrough of the "new form," the "new style," the "new sense of life," the *nouvelle vague*. "We are poets, and we want to get rid of the scientific swindlers, the Marxists, the cold, the shallow, and the spiritless so that poetic vision, the artistically concentrated form, enthusiasm, and prophecy can find the place where henceforth they can do and work and built."[19]

Thus, though it be true that the really creative artist is ordinarily more fulfilled by the idea and its inner vision, which, despite all his efforts, can only be imperfectly incarnated in any form, there are also among these productive geniuses strict ritualists and celebrants of the form, at least during transitional creative periods. This enchantment with the strict form at times takes on the character of an almost compulsive obligation so that the form is experienced literally as the *fanum* and the obsession with form imprints a truly fanatical trait on the artist: inexorable rigor and a compressed compulsive attitude. Even though Stefan George glorifies the inner, organic form-experience in Goethe's sense ("the body deified and the deity bodified"), extrinsic formal legality nevertheless penetrates his verses sometimes in an almost violent way, and he considers it necessary to defend himself against the accusation of being considered the "prince drunk on scented oil" who, "gently rocked, counts his measures." Rilke, during the period of his thing-poems, passed through the phase of form-fascination which pushed him dangerously close to affectation, and Mallarmé only too easily succumbed to this danger.

Of course, in the immediate proximity of such form-fanaticism there is also the danger of a change into complete form-dissolution and form-destruction. With equal passion, with the same stubborn, inexorable consequence the worshipped form is one day smashed to pieces, and then, not infrequently, there begins a furious, chaotic orgy of formlessness, a paroxysm of destruction, or at least a phase of the fluttering-away of forms. Then the followers and worshippers of this art form find themselves bewildered and confused. They may perhaps try to explain such an "unbelievable" event as a psychic-spiritual illness of the artist, an event which Ernst Kretschmer long ago interpreted as being founded in the psychic constitution. The day comes, however, when the same artist once again surprises us with new form-attempts, with a strict, well-composed structure. Kandinski is a good example of this; he suddenly changes from formless "improvisations" that completely diffuse into "wellings and gushings" to "compositions" that present razor-sharp, subtle, and neatly finished "pictures" composed of many geometrical figures.[20] High cubism destroys every closed form in hundreds of fragments, and the fragments of the original gestalt whirl in and out. Later on, with surrealism, there begin to be combinations of the most heterogeneous things, ending with the combinations of the grotesque (Chirico). In music we find similar radical break with all the laws of form of Western tradition. The old tonal system is abandoned for a complete atonality ranging from Debussy to Schön- berg, who strives radically to push through his rationally constructed twelve-tone system. This has finally created "curiosities, such as those of George Antheil, who writes piano compositions in which, alongside the normal ten fingers, the fist and forearm struggle with the piano for expression."[21]

Even among "great men" we can sometimes see the change from highest form-discipline to form-hostility. Hölderlin's pathos-hymnic form-language is bordered on the one side by the restless, confused phase of his late puberty with its chaotic form-decay of throbbing verse and on the other by the late phase of his catatonic schizo- phrenia with a typical form-dissolution. This alternation of phases from form-affirmation to form-negation is also typical of Picasso and Salvador Dali. To what degree here biorhythmical influences play a part deserves a separate and thorough examination. If the fanatic, in the most generalized sense of the term, easily becomes vic- tim of the law of psychic "enantiodromia" (counter- course), then this is even more true of the form-fanatic. At one time the "sacred" value of the form is experi- enced and fashioned, and at another its seductive power and its magically deluding fascination become recognized and are hatefully destroyed; one then seeks to penetrate the "innermost nature" of things in a fanatical idealism.

It is crucial in our context to keep in mind the more
or less fanatical traits of these form-fanatics and especially to take note of the experience of form as a value
evoking fanatical trait. This is also of worth for our
understanding of fanaticism, since we hereby gain the
insight that the purely formalistic fanatic tends toward
a compulsive attitude, toward constriction and violence,
whereas artistic form-fanaticism, along with sublime-
hymnic, can take on the character of the all too construc-
tivistic, the affected, and even grotesquely bizarre—of
course, more to the eye of the "outsider" than to the
form-fanatic himself.

The Fanatic of the Ethical Form—The fanatic of the
ethical form is not the type to whom the ethical value
signifies above all a true, inner imperative, a personal call
—for value is designed in being itself and its realization
therefore establishes a true self-value. Let us clearly
emphasize that what the fanatic of ethical form experiences is external conformity of action with the ethical
form, with the "law." The more exact and complete this
conformity manifests itself the more perfect is the experience of ethical form. Unyielding, integral behavior
according to the strictest standards of the moral code
becomes the supreme value, the *fanum*. Ethical forms
are absolutized and are in the center of thinking, feeling,
and action. Therefore to fulfill the last letter of the moral
code under any circumstances and without exception is

for these types a constant and entirely consuming task. Even authentic inner development and love for a supreme being and fellowman retreat before the force of this obligation. The radical attitude of completely fulfilling the law gives these types, at least consciously, a strong sense of security—an ego-value—or, in case of failure, a heightened sense of inferiority and often a self-tormenting guilt complex. Conceptual rigidity and externality generally drives them into behavior alien to life and reality, since they take isolation from the living present and from the concrete environment in stride with the principle: *fiat justitia, pereat mundus.*

Even though the ethical formalists in any particular instance appeal to the higher motives and greater depths of thinking when one calls their attention to their too rigid attitude, it remains quite difficult for a third person to believe in these higher motives which are expected to give evidence of a great inner vitality and elasticity, for we much more often find here unyielding rigor, cold mechanics, uniform schematics, stubborn dogmatism, and unfeeling literalness. It is quite possible that in the beginning there may have been an inner experience of value, which even later on can time and again be awakened by more profound reflection, but the psychic behavior nevertheless seems decisively determined by the external "attitude," by blameless correctness, and by the standardized "style." The behavior itself is subject to an inner coercion, which however is generally not recognized, since the "higher" motives act as a grandiose and at the same time protective cover-up. The gradual deterioration of an originally deeply stirring and personally absorbing experience into a shallow and empty legalism has on the outsider an almost frightening and repulsive effect. Since the ethical factor manifests itself in most human areas—it is indeed a quality of human existence and behavior in all life situations in all value-creating and value-experiencing realms—many groups of subtypes of the ethical form-fanatic could be enumerated. Here we will mention only three.

In our first group are those ethical form-fanatics who in their *individual* striving attempt to reach the perfect ethical form in a kind of ethical running amok. Psychotherapy generally refers to these as *"perfectionists."*[22] The perfectionist always seeks the most noble, the most pure, the most perfect, and he seeks it in an absolute degree. He cannot stand even the shadow of his own inadequacy and torments himself because of his failure. He is galled by the many limitations, arising externally from his environment and internally from his own limited capacity, which hinder his drive. His ideals are so exaggerated and so little adjusted to reality that he can accept neither himself nor his fellowman. He nags and complains, becomes cynical and succumbs to the manifold forms of a more or less articulated aggressiveness against himself and others. We have only to think of the multitude of great and small perfectionists who embitter their own and other people's lives until they find themselves in a compromising situation: There is the "ideal husband" who makes his marriage the arena of his ethical form-fanaticism and as "head of the family" tyrannizes his wife and children with his draconian rigor and querulousness; there is the boss who indulges in a work-ethos that pushes all his employees into an unhappy, oppressed hustling; there is the "teacher" who practices military discipline in his classes and has no idea how his intimidated pupils compensate for it during their breaks; there is also the preacher who shrinks Christ's happy message into a proclamation of punishment in purgatory and hell and who terrorizes even the ten-year-olds into severe guilt complexes because of "their unworthy reception of the sacraments" and "their unforgivable sins against the Holy Spirit."

The variations are many but they all have in common the one basic trait of perfectionism. The substantives of their vocabulary have a pathetic simplicity, "character," "straight line," "spirit of the whole"; the modifiers: "uncompromising," "entire," "complete," "down-the-line," "absolute," are part of their inventory of stereotyped expressions and scarcely adequate to halfway express what they mean. The rigid insistence on the once-established viewpoint is what gives this type its sense of value. Inflexibility of the decision once made and stubborn adherence to it are seen as supreme values, as "steadfastness of character" and "manliness." All outside resistance makes this attitude only all the more rigid and set. What is peculiar here is that even the motivation for this behavior gradually recedes; the truth or untruth of the reasoning seems no longer to play a role; the only important thing is the insistence of the decision once made. In the heat of battle the only value is the idol of the "never give in," the "under no circumstances weaken." The opponent is mercilessly made suspect, caricatured, played down, gibbeted.

Ibsen put this type on the stage in a unique artistic integrity and impressively depicted the fatal role and destructive power of this attitude in his *Brand*. The idol of ethical formalism, of unbending steadfastness of character to the abandonment of all other human values finds its precise and shocking expression in Brand's words:

> "Be passion's slave, be pleasure's thrall,—
> But be it utterly, all in all!
> Be not to-day, to-morrow, one,
> Another when a year is gone;
> Be what you are with all your heart,
> And not by pieces and in part.
> The Bacchant's clear, defined, complete,
> The sot, his sordid counterfeit;
> Silenus charms; but all his graces
> The drunkard's parody debases.
> Traverse the land from beach to beach,
> Try every man in heart and soul,

You'll find he has no virtue whole,
But just a little grain of each."[23]

If such a perfectionist does not one day fall into the other extreme or if he does not finally find his way to a more moderate, creaturely attitude he may end up in a profound and all-destroying despair. Life then seems meaningless and unbearable since the ideals so uncompromisingly defended cannot be reached. Everything seems to be futile because the supreme value which he has inexorably striven after fails him; perfection is unattainable. Depressions raise their voice; destructive impulses awaken and the danger of suicide becomes acute.

Even in the perfectionist the law of enantiodromia bestirs itself. Then it often happens that the counter-tendencies break through in primitive chaotic forms and the perfectionist—surprisingly to his associates, yet long foreseen by the psychologist—turns into a laxist, perhaps even into a militant amoralist or immoralist. We need only recall that shining example from literature, André Gide (who wrote not only *The Counterfeiters* and *Les Caves du Vatican* but also *Strait Is the Gate,* the intimate song of heavenly love, and *The Pastoral Symphony*).

Within this group of distinct perfectionists we must also put the *fanatics of duty,* who appear quite often, especially in the wake of Kant's ethics of duty. The "categorical imperative," that joyless and listless, almost morose and sullen avowal of obligation was put in its right light by Schiller in his well-known distich:

> "Gladly do I serve the delights, but unfortunately
>   I do it with propensity,
> And thus it vexes me that I am not virtuous."
> "There is no other way! Thou must try to despise
>   them
> And then do it with disgust as duty orders thee."

But the fanatics of a rampant sense of duty do not easily take advice. "Their moral accent is always on the idea of obligation and coercion or of service and self-sacrifice. They allow themselves no rest, have no time to be tired, sacrifice every joy in life, their recreations, their Sunday rest, and expect all others to do the same. There is something tormenting in their sense of duty which can make it a heavy burden for themselves, their family, and their place of work," says Kretschmer in regard to this type of duty fanatic.[24] In this context of an abstract fanatical concept of duty we must also mention certain types of high-ranking military officers who cannot be classified on the lower level of formalistic attitude or hardened-soldier complex since they are motivated by a value-experience of the moral norm and the fulfillment of moral obligations—which, however, they isolate from the total ethical realm and absolutize as the only maxim of their way of life. We cannot fail to mention here the behavior of top generals of the Third Reich between 1939 and 1945.

The ethical form-fanatics whose ethos is very closely

linked with *religious value* are a group unto themselves. Here we find first of all the "pharisees" as described in the New Testament, who always play a great role in the Christian proclamation. Christ's words must, without doubt, be taken to mean that the pharisees have externalized what was perhaps an originally authentic religious concern. He says: "So you also outwardly appear just to men, but within you are full of hypocrisy and iniquity" (Matt. 23:28), and "Blind guides, who strain out the gnat but swallow the camel!" (Matt. 23:24). Therefore the Sermon on the Mount demands a shift from external deeds to an internal way of thought and declares legalism to be not only inadequate but clearly detrimental: "The letter kills, but the spirit gives life."

But the pharisee is not merely a historical phenomenon; he moves with zealous obstinacy through all centuries and time and again inexorably insists on the fulfillment of the letter, the traditions, and the rituals. He is the man who has made a special pact with his God and therefore can no longer open his mouth without having the name of God on his lips. In most instances his God is a God of vengeance, of inflexibility and condemnation, a spiteful, easily offended, and domineering God, a God in whose eyes laughter, song, and dance are crimes worthy of punishment, a censor with a fiery sword who punishes the slightest faults and demands retribution of the children and the children's children till the debt is paid.[25]

For such fanatics all human associations turn into the

last judgment, merciless and terrifying to all whose God is less revengeful since he allows his sun to shine over the good and bad, advising that the weeds be not torn out before the harvest. The question which arises here, of course, is to what extent such pharisees have not themselves been the victims of a close-minded "education" or unconscious self-deceits. After all, who would freely and consciously make a fetish of the letter that kills?

A more naive type of this subgroup—less upsetting than the pharisee yet one whose ethical form-fanaticism is quite obvious and who often creates problems in court —is the conscientious objector to military service. Even though today there are quite a few conscientious objectors who consider war with its modern atomic weapons a very questionable means of defense and of establishing order and who can hardly be called fanatics in every case, it does happen quite often that there are overall pacifistic conceptions—and also religious reasons which confirm the conscientious objector in his fanatic behavior. Court hearings indicate that the guiding principles of these men often consist of a purely literal interpretation of certain biblical passages taken out of context, formed into distinct doctrines, and taken as absolute. Attempts at clarification are often rejected with an astonishing spiritual arrogance. In our section on the psychic backgrounds we will once more deal with this type, since it bears a specific psychic profile.

We can classify as a third subgroup those fanatics

of the ethical form who couple their rigid ethical ideal with *social values* and motives. They are neither individualistic perfectionists nor are they pious pharisees but social utopians who have fanatically raised to the altar the value of absolute "justice for all." Time and again hecatombs of young lives are sacrificed to this idol in concentration camps and forced deportations. It is not snobbishness that this type in particular is so often represented in literature. True, Kleist's Michael Kohlhaas may seem too literary to our modern ideas and experiences. But in *The Just Assassins* Camus cuts through this problem to its ultimate antitheses: Do endless streams of blood have to flow in order to bring about the dawn of justice? Must one become a murderer to realize a more just order? Do millions of people have to be cruelly liquidated, inquisitioned to death in order to fulfill the vision of a "kingdom of justice"? Inhuman purging procedures are regularly part of a system overrun with totalitarian tendencies of a political or spiritual character. Friedrich Dürrenmatt also deals with this problem in *Die Ehe des Herrn Mississippi* (The Marriage of Mr. Mississippi). The public prosecutor works himself up into a delusion of justice that cold-bloodedly takes every murder in stride. Saint-Claude reproaches him: "We have both shed blood, you have killed three hundred and fifty criminals and I have never counted my victims. What we are doing is murder and therefore we must do it meaningfully. You acted in the name of God and I in the name of communism. My deed is better than yours for I want something in time and you want something in eternity. The world is not in need of salvation from sin but must be saved from hunger and oppression. . . ."

It is a fact that fanatics of justice always have a "law" according to which the enemy must die. The enemy must be liquidated, for he strips from the fanatic of justice his right of psychic-spiritual existence in that he relativizes his *fanum,* the sacred value of the absolutely just order. As is well-known, the courts have often to deal with cases of private justice, even of murder committed in the delusion of justice. Seldom do these "just" ever get the idea that absolute justice cannot be realized on this earth without causing the greatest injustices. If it ever should happen, then a catharsis would perhaps take place and a better adjustment to reality.

But also in this group an inner "change" can occur, similar to that among the fanatics of the artistic form. A bitterness takes hold of the man against a world in which absolute justice is impossible. Fanatics of perfection then turn into rebels and nihilists, types who are depicted in striking colors by Dostoevski (*The Possessed,* Ivan in *The Brothers Karamazov*) and who in the reality of concrete everyday life can be met in various guises, from the little salesgirl to the famous scientist and artist; they all harden into an unyielding, sterile protest.

To this subgroup also belong the refractory and tenacious types generally called *"querulous."* They never get over an actual or seeming injustice but lament and accuse and finally bring it to court. They appeal from one court to another and finally even attack their own lawyers. They accuse the judges of plotting against them, of having a vicious and hostile attitude, and finally come to threats and violence. The querulous individual can ordinarily never be convinced concerning the injustice of his own accusation. He disregards his own damage and the misery brought on his family, sacrifices all his time and energy for one purpose: to be right and to have his right recognized. G. Anton gives us a brief and striking description of the querulous: "A seeming or real miscarriage of justice causes an exaggerated reaction in him, or, so to speak, an aggressive spasm; he freezes into a fighting stance and becomes inapproachable to balancing thoughts, feelings, and motives. The really or apparently persecuted now becomes a pathological persecutor."[26] Are not these and similar types to be found always and everywhere? And do not they, too, belong in the great album of the many little fanatics?

In this group also we find the ordinary *zealots* who only momentarily, like a lightning flash, let their fanatically seething psychic ground flare up, again in the name of some ideal or of some term: "The liberal, humanitarian, progressive August Forel becomes in his Order of Good Templars . . . intolerant and fanatic. It is known that he once succeeded by means of physical force in making a drunkard take a vow of abstinence."[27] This merely exemplifies how, for the sake of the "purity of an idea" one can utterly reject this very idea, strange as this may seem.

Summarizing our discussion of this group of fanatics we can point to some valuable conclusions: While the types of a merely formalistic value-attitude can be understood even without the relationship to value, that is, merely based on their subjective psychic mentality, the form-fanatics if separated from their object-relationship—their clearly profiled value-attitude—would not be adequately represented, even in their concrete manifestation, for value-attitude is part of them and impregnates their behavior. This impression becomes even stronger when we consider that in the particular case it is only the individual, specific, concrete value which can awaken, increase and maintain fanatic intensity of behavior over a long period of time, whereas other values are unimportant or of merely secondary interest because of their relationship to the dominant value. The form-fanatic in the artistic realm would not be willing to spend proportionate energy to act in accordance with ethical norms, and, conversely, the ethical form-fanatic generally cannot comprehend an excessive use of energy for the aesthetic perfection of a work. Exceptions—we may think here, for instance, of Van Gogh's religious, social, and artistic perfectionism—can hardly be understood without focusing on the background of fanatic value-attitude.

The form-fanatics of the various value realms are rightly seen by their fellowmen in a different light than are the merely formalistic types of fanatics. But the difference is important since it lies, beyond all intensity, in the value-attitude. The fanaticism of this group-type is rooted in a greater depth of the personal structure than it is in the formalists (where the term "person" is not favored) and therefore has more impact on the psychic totality.

Thus the separation of fanatics into these groups from the viewpoint of value-attitude seems both justified and fruitful.

3. Types of Intrinsic Value-content

The Intrinsic Antinomy between Value-attitude and Fanaticism—Is there also a third group of fanatics, who have an authentic, intrinsic, and even creative relationship to a specific value-content manifested either as an inner form inseparably joined with the content or as central idea and value? This question seems superflous, even incomprehensible if one considers that this is the very fanatic who intervenes in history as a revolutionary social reformer—for instance, Marx or Lenin—or who makes decisive thrusts in the religious realm—like Calvin or Savonarola—or who not so much programmatically as creatively helps in giving birth to a new theory of art—such as some of the great painters and sculptors of the Renaissance and the Baroque era.

Nevertheless the question is not only justified but necessary, since with it the problem of fanaticism becomes most acute. An intrinsic value-relationship requires psychic properties that are hard to connect with the properties of fanaticism for they are largely in opposition. Later we will have to deal more thoroughly with this opposition, but we wish first to characterize this opposition with the statement that an intrinsic value-relationship demands great receptive, productive power, whereas fanaticism, at least outer-directed fanaticism, is ordinarily aggressive-destructive in its effects and originates in a psychically unbalanced and at times even quite brittle situation.

What makes our theme as difficult as it is fascinating is the fact that some fanatic geniuses are neither "merely fanatics" nor "merely inspired." They are not "merely fanatics," since they have the central inner experience of an original relationship to the specific value-content. Obviously, however, he who from the very start considers every creative intoxication and creative ecstasy, every enthusiasm for an idea, every self-consuming zeal for a new social order or for the "kingdom of God" as only a pathological exaggeration, a monomania, or a substitute for repressed instincts is not capable of viewing this phenomenon in the right light. On the other hand, neither are these zealots and fighters exclusively the "merely inspired," pure enthusiasts and "martyrs" for an idea. The fanatical character, the obsession that blindly rushes headlong and brutally liquidates all resistance, which is desired almost as much as it is hated, should not be explained away as a harmless side phenomenon. In this type it is a matter of recognizing the strange coupling of very contradictory qualities. Every attempt to weaken this contrast, yes, even contradiction—let alone seek to bring it into harmony by twisting the facts—automatically blocks the way to understanding.

Of course the distinct levels of the particular value must be taken into consideration. Even though in the individual case very slight values appear important and almost essential, a disregard of the value-attitude may nevertheless be justified when it is a matter of fanatic stamp collectors, bicyclists, or fanatic jazz fans and vegetarians, since in these cases a preference for such "values" is generally considered arbitrary and inconsistent. But in fanatic geniuses and the historically important fanatics the function of what is called value is so unique and decisive that our disregard of it would make the total situation of these fanatics incomprehensible. Here the question once more presents itself in its entire import: Is it the content, the ideas, and the values which work as an enormously accelerating and overwhelming motor, or is it the psychic condition which empowers the intensity of experience and sends it into top speed? It is clear that on this level of value-attitude the phenomenology of type is correspondingly more complicated and the illumination of the psychic background more difficult. For the present we will here again deal merely with the concrete manifestation of this type.

The Type in General—Despite its fanaticism this type shows the qualities of a true value-attitude. This is due in part, of course, to the fact that the value has not been received merely from the outside through a purely suggestive influence, for example, through education, through one's cultural environment, or by injunction. We find rather a strong intrinsic value-experience based on a structurally rooted, primitive relationship to a value. The value-content is interiorly experienced and deeply integrated in the structure of the person. The criteria for the existence of this inner value-relationship seem to be the following:[28] There is a need for personal value which for years and decades, in a strong and systematic drive for value-experience, seeks to arrive at a subjective stimulation by value and at a psychic value-fulfillment and by this to achieve as goal a new value-realization and value-intensification in the objective, extrapersonal, and suprapersonal realm. Such a drive for value-experience clearly distinguishes itself from every kind of stimulus hunger and from a mere delight in sensation which simply strives for an always newly stimulated state of one's subjectivity and thus for self-gratification. This drive likewise distinguishes itself from an unconscious-instinctive, blind "being forced" by its clear value-insight and conscious value-striving.

It should be obvious that in saying this we do not wish to overlook, let alone to reject, the archetypal foundation of the collective unconscious, which Jung has convincingly pointed out especially in respect to the process of creativity.[29] But the part played by conscious mental activity in this context should be given equal consideration. Arguing from a comprehensive study of this matter, Julius Bahle says emphatically: "It is not coincidence, arbitrariness, and irregularity that characterize the creative person but his organic discipline and tenacity of purpose. Not the 'unconscious' but the value-conscious is what is actually creative in the artist. Not the 'demonic' but the active value-bond of the artist demands application, direction, and goal in creation and gives the artist the resemblance of something demonic, which at its climax we would call value-obsession."[30]

Even a healthy and strong striving for intrinsic value is quite in agreement with this value-attitude, although the character of transcending into the objective world of values imprints this experience with the stamp of a transient striving.[31] Here the mightily active engagement manifests itself in an almost wild though generally periodic work-enthusiasm which is marked, on the one hand, by a concentration of all psychic functions excluding all distraction and indifference and, on the other, by a value-knowing and value-choosing selection which methodically singles out a very specific object and places it at the center of experience. We especially notice in this a quality that seems extremely important for distinguishing the nonfanatic value-attitude from the fanatic, namely the unprejudiced, great attitude of inquiry[32] which is not restricted but seeks to thrust through to the core and therefore leads, step by step, more deeply into the realm of value. This attitude of inquiry opens up all the gates of the senses and of the soul and keeps them open to new searching and striving. A psychic expansion takes place, urging to action and giving a sense of value-fulfillment.

In the fanatic genius this authentic value-attitude now joins other qualities which at first intensify the picture and give it an even more fascinating appearance but at the same time confuse and make it incomprehensible, even contradictory. The power of concentration grows to an exaggerated, feverish intensity of action and an uncanny sharpening of the external performance of the conditions of its realization. The affective accompaniment is played fortissimo or in a long-lasting crescendo. At the same time—and here is the step into fanaticism— the vision and the universal attitude of inquiry become more and more restricted, and this restriction sets up a contrast to the original broadness and unlimitedness of the value-attitude. The outsider gradually gets the impression of a fixated rigor and inflexible stubbornness. The fanatic genius feels himself even less understood than before; he believes himself misunderstood and despised in his most sacred world of experience. His feelings then abreact with aggressive intolerance and his enemies are accused of being philistine, boorish or godless. Finally this can lead to complete identification with a more and more isolated partial value which is increasingly absolutized as the supreme and only value.

Thus two contradicting tendencies clash within the innermost psychic realm: the dynamics of the value-drive with its universal and open attitude of inquiry and the dynamics of a persistent but restricted view with its aggressive intolerance. The fanatic genius hereby reveals himself as an individual of a profound inner contrast, even of a fatal split. This interior discord of his own affect-tendencies results in the discharge of aggression toward the outside or in self-tormenting, masochistic depressions. This is bound to lead to a sterile formalism claiming infallibility or to a destructive rage, states which can still be interrupted by "healthy" intervals with above-average achievements and even accomplishments of genius.[33]

This third type of fanatic is, without doubt, the most significant and psychologically the most interesting. But due to his paradoxical mixture of the value-inspiration of genius and monomanic one-sidedness it will always be difficult to see the point where these traits meet and where, without paralyzing each other, they form an almost indissoluble unity. At one time he will appear to be more the fanatic *enthusiast* who rampages in "storm and stress," exhausts himself in the ecstasy of his enthusiasm, and is inundated by his pleasure in work, who in his

long-term states of psychic fermentation finally loses
sight of all other values and completely disregards his
fellowmen and their welfare and even his own health and
reputation—and at another time he will appear as the
hard, inflexible, even brutal *fighter* who in the name of
a high ideal coldly and sullenly destroys his enemy; like
a "sleepwalker" he stares ahead to his ideal, namely a
more just and better world order. This has been the
behavior of all world-betterers, whether they have sword
in hand like Alexander the Great, Caesar, and Napoleon,
or use fire or guillotine like the inquisitors and Robespierre, or sit at their desk turning out fiery manifestos
or endless theses as did Karl Marx in the sociopolitical
realm and Sören Kierkegaard in the religious.[34]

The Type in Particular: Enthusiasts—An especially
impressive example of the enthusiastic value-fanatic can
be found in Vincent van Gogh. He stands on the borderline between the open and sublime value-attitude of the
creative artist and the wild and reckless eruptions of
fanatic protest and constricted monomanic one-sidedness. We have many testimonies of his inner contradiction. His letters to his brother indicate both the gradiose
scope of the value-drive as it makes the highest demands
and, simultaneously, a constriction of consciousness
which quickly reproaches others with dishonest half-
measures, narrow philistinism, and compromising tendencies. Like few other creative artists Van Gogh knew

how to express in these letters[35] the highest will to value, the enthusiastic pleasure in work which not only animates the artist but thrusts him forward:

"I do not know myself how I paint it. I sit down with a white board before the spot that strikes me, I look at what is before my eyes, I say to myself, That white board must become something; I come back dissatisfied—I put it away, and when I have rested a little, I go and look at it with a kind of fear. Then I am still dissatisfied, because I still have that splendid scene too clearly in my mind to be satisfied with what I made of it. But I find in my work an echo of what struck me, after all. I see that nature has told me something, has spoken to me, and that I have put it down in shorthand. In my shorthand there may be words that cannot be deciphered, there may be mistakes or gaps; but there is something of what wood or beach or figure has told me in it, and it is not the tame or conventional language derived from a studied manner or a system rather than from nature itself" (vol. I, p. 448). "There is something infinite in painting —I cannot explain it to you so well—but it is so delightful just for expressing one's feelings. There are hidden harmonies or contrasts in colors which involuntarily combine to work together and which could not possibly be used in another way" (I, 441).

"You need a certain dose of inspiration, a ray from on high, that is not in ourselves, in order to do beautiful things" (III, 253). "And if, frustrated in the physical power, a man tries to create thoughts instead of children, he is still part of humanity. And in a picture I want to say something comforting, as music is comforting. I want to paint men and women with that something of the eternal which the halo used to symbolize, and which we seek to convey by the actual radiance and vibration of our coloring" (III, 25). "But I prefer painting people's eyes to cathedrals, for there is something in the eyes that is not in the cathedral, however solemn and imposing the latter may be—a human soul, be it that of a poor beggar or of a streetwalker, is more interesting to me" (II, 462).

Yet at the same time in combination with this extremely broad and profoundly true value-attitude overflowing with enthusiasm, are peculiarities which not only reveal a man "charged with electricity," but indicate a close proximity to fanatic excess, to stubbornly restricted affectivity and monomanic exclusiveness. Fanatic tendencies, lurking in many psychic structures, often prevail in Van Gogh—without at first being able to pull him completely into their wake, since his productive drive for value-creation time and again shows its balancing and almost therapeutic effect. But in Arles (1888–89) exuberant impulses more and more chase one another into a wild raging. He himself says: "It's the only time I feel I am alive, when I am drudging away at my work. If I had company, I should feel it less of a necessity; or rather I'd work at more complicated things. But alone, I only count on the exaltation that comes to me at certain moment, and then I let myself run to extravagances" (II, 600).

Yet Van Gogh was always possessed by this mania of extremes. Already as a missionary in the Borinage he had beaten himself with a club, slept on the floor, abstained from meat, and on one occasion he threw his silver watch into the collection-basket, and on another his gloves. His first day there he gave away not only his clothes and his money but covered his face with soot in order to be as much as possible like the mine workers. When, as a result of his behavior, the Evangelical mission society decided to dismiss him, he worked himself up into a fury against the Church, in which, he said, one becomes "calloused and petrified," and he even considered the "whole system of this worship of God detestable" and "the traditional concepts of God, men, moral, and virtue, balderdash."

". . . The whole university, the theological faculty at least, is, in my eyes, an inexpressible mess, a breeding place of Pharisaism" (II, 146). "But for heaven's sake, what is the meaning of that standing and of that religion which the respectable people maintain?—oh, they are perfectly *absurd,* making society a kind of lunatic asylum, a perfectly topsy-turvy world" (II, 304).

We know how much this deeply value-conscious artist could lose himself in a state of fury, even against his best friends and how terrible was his consequent need of expiation. On one occasion, after he had thrown a bottle at Gauguin's head, he cut off his own ear, wrapped it in paper and took it to the brothel. Here the pathological admixture is unmistakable, but it is interesting that the form of his illness could never be diagnosed with complete certitude.[36] Our purpose here is merely to show the strange mixture of true value-attitude and fanatic character traits which in the case of Van Gogh led to an unbearable inner tension. Yet many great persons have manifested a similar opposition in the psychic structure: artists such as Michelangelo, Beethoven, Wagner; political figures—Cromwell, Napoleon, Lenin; religious reformers—Wycliff, Müntzer, and many others.

III. BACKGROUNDS OF THE FANATIC VALUE-ATTITUDE

In the beginning of this chapter we emphasized that the self-concept of the fanatic should not be overlooked or underestimated. Many fanatics perceive themselves as men of significant value-experience and of an intense value-forming drive which pushes them to the fullest expenditure of their psychic and vital energy potential. Our typology of fanatic value-attitudes should have made it clear that certain groups of fanatics (especially the "great" fanatics) must be understood, at least in part, from the viewpoint of their value-attitude. This position clearly rejects Stertz's opinion that the content of fanatic idea-orientation is of "subordinate importance in comparison to the form of the supporting frame of mind."[37] We must nevertheless go behind even this value-attitude as a fulfillment of the meaning of existence and seek backgrounds for it and for its exaggeration. For even in these cases value-attitude is not always the ultimate and only explanation of fanatic behavior (with the exception of the view of our first chapter) and in many cases the impulse factor of value-attitude is combined with other driving forces that condition fanaticism. Thus fanaticism more and more manifests itself as compexly determined, even as the expression of a distinct psychophysical and spiritually value-bound total situation of man whereby the decisive element in the formation of fanaticism can be different in each individual case. The psychology of the unconscious speaks of hidden undercurrents whenever suspiciously disproportioned behavior becomes evident. When we investigate the value-attitude of the fanatic from this viewpoint we come face to face once more with the category of compensation and indeed in quite diverse forms. There is also another phenomenon which needs mentioning and which often plays a very important role in this connection but which we will not go into at this point because of its complexity, namely the fanatic's consciousness of election and mission and his drive for the absolute. Here we must limit ourselves to a closer consideration of the character of compensation in the fanatic's value-attitude.

1. VALUE-FANATICISM AS COMPENSATION

At this point it is no longer a matter of viewing the fanatic *intensity* of value-attitude as compensation but rather the value-attitude itself, the personal reaction to a value, the readiness for value-experience and the value-forming drive. Fanatic intensity, of course, plays its role, but here the fanatic value-attitude itself is the means of compensation. Thus the choice of a specific value and its profession must be understood not only as a spontaneous effect of natural dispositions and tendencies but also as compensation, and even more, the compensatory character of the value-attitude in these cases presses almost by necessity to fanaticism.

Without doubt, in view of the multilayered character of human activity and its many psychic processes a keen eye can almost always discover compensatory traits. This fact, however, neither allows us to ignore these traits nor, at the other extreme, to take a "nothing-but-compensation" viewpoint. Certainly there are "confessions" of creative individuals which at times tempt one to take the latter stand; but a more thorough reflection on the person and his work generally shows the transitional character of such statements. For example, Richard Wagner once wrote to Franz Liszt: "I cannot understand how a truly happy person can get the idea to create art. . . . Art is a confession of impotence. . . ." More serious is the statement of Kujath maintaining that the fanatic lacks the "natural and unproblematic being-in-

the-world, which explains why in some cases the formation of pseudoscientific philosophical systems comes to
pass."[38] Is there such a thing as an unproblematic being-
in-the-world for a mentally alert individual? Is not
human existence simply *the* central problem so that the
question of finding a fulfilling value as the meaning of
life necessarily imposes itself on everyone who lives more
than a day to day existence and who experiences the
fluctuating relationship with his environment?

The need of value is not in itself a compensation phenomenon; it must be recognized in the function basic to
human existence. It is structure-rooted and universally
human, since man's spirituality and its transcendence-
dynamics acknowledges and strives for ever new values.
The fact that this need of value can be more and more
subjected also to compensatory purposes can influence
and falsify its original meaning, but it can never make
it completely forgotten. The compensation mechanism
may then urge to the production of values—yet its rank
and radiating power is determined by the creative capacity of the person. Bahle rightly says that "so-called
'human weaknesses' become creative forces only when
they participate as forms of dynamic drives *together* with
the product-determining experiences in the realization
of ideal values. . . ." "The value of a piece of art is
always determined not only by these forms of dynamic
drive but also by the mentality, the value-substance, and
the talent of the creative personality; for these determine

in the first place *what* is created, whereas the dynamic drives mainly see to it *that* creation takes place. Seen in this light the quite egotistical and status-connected drives are at no time reprehensible or inartistic but perform an activating and achievement-enhancing function in the development and creative work of every artistic personality."[39] Only a materialistic weltanschaungsdogma can see the restlessly intensive involvement in a higher value as purely compensatory in every case.

The exaggeration of the need of value, so evident in fanatic traits, may indicate a compensatory background, but equally often it must be viewed as based on constitutional, monomanic character traits.[40]

On the other hand a purely negative, blindly raging hostility against a value or against the representative of a value can almost unfailingly be recognized as compensatory. This happens, for instance, when, using every ounce of energy, one equips a "scapegoat" with every possible hateful trait and fights against him with obsessive fury. The tendency to interpose such scapegoats is quite universal and depth psychology is right in seeing it as a projection of an unconscious inferiority. In daily life, in the family, in school, business, political party, sports, etc., everywhere we look, this projection mechanism plays the part of a universal defense mechanism. Yet it does not reach a fanatic degree and keeps within bounds. But in troubled periods of transition it attains the heights of intensity and can grow into a fanatic mass delusion. The end of the medieval era with its persecution of the Jews, its superstition regarding heretics and witches exemplifies this collective fanatic character and at the same time reveals by this its underlying insecurity, the masses' threatened sense of life in premonition of the dawn of a new era. It was in the period following World War I when political revolutions and never-ending economic crises had created a general insecurity affecting a greater part of the population that in Germany national socialism, not without success, could make the Jews the universal scapegoat, cultivate artificial hatred, and never cease fanning its fire. That Hitler's attitude toward the Jewish problem is an exact illustration of an overwhelming and completely numbing compensatory attitude is best proved by the fact that his blind hatred of the Jews was not only with him from his youth but had developed into a psychic "necessity" that enabled him to shift the blame for every failure and have a label ready for every danger.

Fanatic value-negation and value-destruction are hardly thinkable without the mechanism of compensation.

Thus we cannot dispense with the concept of compensation but must make careful use of it whenever it seems to open up a background. Yet we must once more be reminded that this term is used in various connotations.[41] In its most general definition as "reaction to a deficiency" it is so inexact as to be scientifically useless. There are above all two functions of compensation which are significant for the purpose of our investigation: the compensatory value as an *ersatz*-value for an absent object-value relationship or for a lack of personal value and, next, the compensatory value as an *escape*-value insofar as it is intended to be a way out of an inner disharmony —a conscious or unconscious screening, a camouflage of a disturbing and threatening id-layer. These forms of compensatory value-attitude must be taken into consideration as background of fanatic value-attitude.

2. COMPENSATORY VALUE AS ERSATZ-VALUE

The value-attitude can serve as ersatz for various human deficiencies and needs. Thus even purely *physical defects* and weaknesses are often compensated for with much effort in a value-area. It can take place primarily within a quite sensible and authentic value-attitude, for example, when even a Beethoven (along with many others) says: "In spite of all weaknesses of the body my spirit shall rule."[42] Such a value-attitude becomes disagreeable and pathological only when it leads to exaggerated counterpositions, to fanatic anti-attitudes as sometimes happens in the case of antidrinkers, antismokers, vegetarians, and racial fanatics. In the great fanatics we often find compensation for somatic defects and nervous symptoms: Savonarola is reported to have had a speech disorder in his youth, and we have already mentioned Calvin's physical debility. The teacher Huber with his fanatic sense of mission, concerning which

Muralt writes in detail, came from a family in which six of ten children died at an early age; he himself was extremely fragile, a delicate mother's boy, had undergone a goiter operation, and manifested obviously homosexual traits in his feminine behavior.[43]

That *unsatisfied instinctual needs* seek compensatory substitutes in a value-attitude was known long before depth psychology. The by no means always voluntary bachelorhood of some geniuses (Beethoven, Bruckner, Schubert, Hölderlin, Nietzsche, Kierkegaard, Van Gogh) is conspicuous and has often been seen by these persons themselves as a defect which could be borne only through an enhanced and extreme value-attitude. What Van Gogh wrote to his brother is a more than clear expression of what many others felt and sensed: ". . . and if, frustrated in the physical power, a man tries to create thoughts instead of children, he is still part of humanity."[44]

Compensation of the *power drive* by intellectual and religious values is also a well-recognized fact. It is expressed quite obviously in phrases employed as propaganda slogans, such as "knowledge is power," or "piety has many advantages." The compensation very easily leads to overcompensation and fanatic behavior. Time and again the lower social classes (and the asocial along with them) are called upon in the name of "freedom" or of a true "humanity" to fight against their "oppressors," and yet how natural it seems to be to these fighters for greater freedom and these benefactors of humanity that consequently hundreds of thousands of individuals are forced into a new slavery or that the "intellectuals" are unscrupulously liquidated. Every revolution without exception can be examined as to this fact and the results are ever the same, namely, that the ideology is betrayed in the struggle for power. Yet we need not refer only to great examples in history; everyday life clearly demonstrates this same law in miniature. The one whose regular course remains blocked in some area easily becomes a rebel against the "system," a militant of a "better order," or at least a fanatic follower and fellow fighter for some kind of "life reform" movement, which, of course, is always and everywhere overdue. But after a short time this "new order" also proves itself unsatisfactory and a still younger generation has already entered the struggle and seeks to "come to power." Not even the supreme value of love escapes this strange perversion grounded in the power drive. There is no greater power than love. Thus almost by necessity we also find fanatics of love and nonviolence—Fénélon, Tolstoi, Gandhi, and many others—who endlessly and profoundly argue about the nature of love and power while having to reckon with the fact that in the course of this procedure love quietly fades away and only dogmatism and obduracy remain.

The complex apparatus of the mechanism of compensation has been so clearly demonstrated by depth psychology that the brief demonstrations we have given here should be sufficient.

That a formalistic value-attitude is quite often merely an ersatz for the lack of an authentic value-relationship has already been intimated in our discussion of value types such as the "professional warriors," activists, and also of certain quack dialecticians. They all lack the capability of a true experience; an interior void pushes them toward emphatic external compensation. It is quite meaningful that, concerning conscientious objectors—not all but quite a few of them—it must be said that they are "intellectually underdeveloped, weak characters who cannot be considered fully responsible," that they have "a need to play the martyr role," and when "a few passages of the Bible are absolutized" a "surprising spiritual arrogance" becomes observable in them, an "absolutely uneducable fanaticism."[45]

3. COMPENSATORY VALUE AS ESCAPE-VALUE

It seems reasonable to distinguish escape-values from ersatz-values. Escape-values are not a matter of a conscious or semiconscious substitution for personal defects or lack of opportunity but of an escape from conflicts, a flight from severe psychic tensions, disharmonies, and splittings. Such tensions are found either in those who did not experience a sheltered atmosphere in their childhood and youth, whose primordial confidence was exposed to doubts and disappointments at an early age, or in those who are almost torn asunder by a multitude of psychic antitheses and interests. In both instances it is very difficult to build an ego-structure capable of sustaining the inner polar tensions and of forming them into a positive unity. This makes an integral and personal confrontation with a fulfilling and development-enhancing value very problematic. In any situation the inner dissociation allows only a partial contact, be it of the mind or of the feelings, with the value. Thus this value can hardly unfold in its depth and fullness. Being capable of merely partial participation leads in certain instances almost necessarily to a compulsive intensification and exaggeration of the value-attitude. This damaged self-confidence, lack of self-possession, and the impossibility of self-assertion force a person to cling to a value schema which is expected to enable him to master life's insecurity and provide protection from existential fear and its frequently accompanying melancholy.

Pertinent here are the seemingly strange exaggerations of Sören Kierkegaard, who was well aware of his primary defect, namely his lack of a basic psychic trust (the result of a disturbed parental relationship). He says: "In terrible inner suffering I became a writer."[46] When he goes on to say: "I need the magic of productivity in order to forget all the paltry details,"[47] we indeed know that his life was not a matter of "paltry details." His relationship with his very old father, the breaking of his engagement with Regina Olsen, and his uncertain position in his profession ("every time when he, who had long passed his examinations, wanted to become a pastor something

always prevented it"[48]) remained neuralgic points in his
life and led to that desperate struggle for the possibility
of his human and Christian existence. His attempt to get
his feet on the ground, his analyses of fear and despair
penetrate the ultimate layers of existence. Yet he was
never allowed to find his place in shelter. His violent
pushing and impatient knocking on the gates of life here
below and life beyond was ever the distressed cry of the
fugitive. Kierkegaard exemplifies most impressively how
an original value-drive can be also combined with a
compensatory component and fuse with it into an almost
indissoluble union.

On a much deeper level are the value fanatics whose
escape-compensation is stronger than the value-creating
impulse. Hindrances to a healthy self-development, constant suffering from an inner uprootedness and insecurity
lead to agonizing and self-tormenting probing, to futile
problemizings and to a querulous and cranky behavior.
From time to time a bursting-out from this unsatisfying
condition becomes due and almost perforce takes on
fanatic degrees. Religious fanatics then become intoxi-
cated with their own religious intolerance and their self-
sacrificing zeal, with their razor-sharp either-or. Religion
becomes the monster strikingly analyzed by Bernhard
Welte: the means are absolutized, given infinite proportion, and inhumanly sharpened in their execution,
whereas the true religious goal, God himself, and the living contact with him is more and more pushed into the

background.[49] In such a situation religious activity takes on the compulsive and addictive character so often observable in the recently converted, whereas in the great "converts" (Paul, Augustine, Ignatius of Loyola) it gradually returns to a more quiet way of down-to-earth service and self-controlled reserve.

The compensatory value-attitude gives evidence of its escape character also in those cases where it functions as a screen against a repressed id-layer. It can then be intensified in such a way that it works like a magic charm. It is important that we recall here how much the contents of the unconscious differ from those of the conscious since they are carefully withheld from this conscious and thus cannot be influenced by it. But they have their own dynamics and thus threaten the conscious ego, from behind, since, according to the law of countercourse (so much stressed by C. G. Jung), they try to establish their counterposition and to enable it to break through. Although the conscious ego seldom senses the danger facing it, nevertheless, it instinctively redoubles its efforts and fortifies its own position, which, of course, also urges the unconscious contents to a stronger conglomeration and complex-formation. A competitive struggle begins between the two rivals, each inciting the other almost to the point of exhaustion.

This struggle can take place in the secret depths of the innerpsychic realm, even though it manifests itself in many neurotic symptoms and leads to an unnecessary

waste of energies. From that psychic function which most
participates in the fanatic value-compensation we can
infer which are the corresponding repressed contents in
the id-layer. In cases where we meet a fanatically *spiritual* value viewpoint which intransigently and dogmati-
cally, blindly and stubbornly fights for its own conviction
we are seldom wrong in assuming that behind such
fanaticism is an equally strong, though mostly unconscious, doubt in this very conviction. C. G. Jung says
concisely that fanaticism is "nothing but overcompensated doubts."[50] We have already quoted the passage
of Savonarola's final sermon where he rages with a violence unusual even for him while at the same time constantly making objections to himself. They are objections
that touch his ultimate inner attitude and can hardly be
interpreted as a rhetorical style of his time or as a scholastic method, but rather as the uncovering of a psychic
ground in which his unconscious reveals contents which
had been repressed time and again. The more such
doubts rankle and torment and the more they keep trying
to cross the threshold of consciousness, the more stubbornly must one hold on to the "conviction" for which
one fights and the less is he willing to seek finer distinctions and conciliatory formulations.

In a similar way the analyst constantly experiences
that behind the will-spasms of a fanatically voluntaristic
moralism, opposing inner instincts and stirrings are
repressed. Instead of striving for a calm and confident

control of these instincts, one rigorously strives for an ideal that can be achieved only in a gradual, painful, and patient effort. Here, too, the fanatic impetus of the rigorist must kill with its overpowering temptations the inner enemy and the laxism of unrestraint, but it will never be successful. With inhuman severity against himself one tries to immobilize the guilt feelings even as they arise and ward off the anxiety, the necessary consequence of repressions.

More often, however, it will not be a matter of overcompensation for an intellectual doubt in one's own ideology but of compensating for a deeper doubt in one's own ego, an inner insecurity and nagging distrust in the value of one's own person. This existential doubt demands perhaps even more effective ersatz activity than does doubt in the truth of a philosophical system, and it tries to produce compensatory experiences equal in importance to those produced by doubt in the truth of religious faith. Hereby one attempts to cover over with value-strivings and value-experiences—and at times with mere value-professions—the neurotic core-condition which has never allowed the development of a relatively harmonious ego aware of its powers. We may call to mind Nietzsche's Zarathustra forcing him to admit to himself: "Now that which has hitherto been your ultimate danger has become your ultimate refuge" (Part III). Did not Richard Wagner have a similarly profound insight into his own interior when he said: "Art is not a psychic luxury but originates in the tormenting pressure of psychic *self-preservation;* this is possible only with enormous *compensations of phantasy.*"[51] He says that he consequently feels good only when he is in a state of ecstatic enthusiasm: "I can live only in extremes." Even the "ideal" Friedrich Schiller knew such inner experiences. He once wrote: "Believe me, one can be wrong, one can see as strength of spirit which ultimately is despair."

Quite often, however, such screening does not continue as an innerpsychic mechanism, but, through the projection of the inner contradiction to the outside world, to real or imagined enemies, it seeks an even more effective camouflage of the enemy in one's own self. The powerful intensities of hatred and aggression, of dogmatism and stubbornness which then rage out of control give an idea of how tremendous the interior struggle would have to be if a portion of this interior were not entirely shut off. It may happen, of course, that this interior suddenly awakens and its contents powerfully come to the fore. Often enough such an event is indicative of psychosis. Or it may be that these contents present themselves as great "archetypal" figures or motives and take possession of the psyche. When this happens they often take a dangerously primordial shape, which is possible only because these contents have never undergone a clarification, an ordering and differentiation, and hence they become extremely virulent and devastating forces within the psyche.

CHAPTER THREE

The Pathology of Fanaticism

In the first two chapters we tried to view the phenomenon of fanaticism from two very different basic aspects. We discovered many differentiations of fanatic types which, though correctly called fanatic, often have little in common in the rest of their psychic profile. Fanaticism is quite possible in numerous psychic contexts and cannot develop merely out of a single "functional construct" or a single "life-design." The problem would be greatly simplified were it possible to clearly understand and classify fanaticism, at least from the pathological viewpoint. But this possibility no longer exists if we seriously consider fanaticism in its multiplicity of forms and types, as we have demonstrated.

The fact alone that fanaticism in some instances may be merely a partial component of secondary importance, a single trait of the person in his totality, and, vice versa, may be manifested as the core and center of a pathological character should make us extremely cautious. Moreover the coupling of fanaticism with the value-attitude seems to make the problem even more serious, since this coupling can fulfill an authentic value-need and even a personal meaning, while on the other hand it often unconsciously uses value as ersatz or even consciously as camouflage. Also the strange readiness of the fanatic to give himself to the very ultimate for "his people," "his homeland," "his religion," while he simultaneously experiences in this his most sublime self-assertion, indicates the very complex character of the fanatic.

These many faces of the fanatic must be taken into account since they characterize him as an individual of a profound inner contradiction and in certain cases even of many contradictions. Therefore it is difficult to order fanaticism into a specific pathological picture. Horstmann correctly called fanaticism the "area of psychic border-states."[1] The healthy and the sick, the value-seeking and the value-rejecting, selfless idealism and brutal cynicism, sensitivity and coldest insensitivity, piety and cruelty, ardent creative drive and senseless will for destruction are often so closely intertwined that only a trained eye can avoid being deceived. But even the trained and experienced eye of the analytical psychologist often finds it difficult to decide in the individual case the transition point of these contrasts. At times, however, it is the fanaticism itself which marks the point where the "still normal" ends and the "already abnormal" begins.

Another difficulty involved in the discussion of the pathology of this phenomenon is the fact that the clinical terms which perforce must be used are merely collective names. They encompass a multiplicity of similar but in each case different pathological symptoms, hereby giving a lead to partial understanding but hardly capable of doing justice in the individual case. Terms are important, but they are meaningfully applied only when one is aware of their limited competency. The layman expects and assumes that clinical terms are reliable labels for a fact which can be precisely indicated. But it is rare that today's science can fulfill this expectation, since the complicated psycho-physical and psycho-spiritual contexts generally make a complete clarification impossible. What is more, some scientists are greatly tempted to create their own terms in order to improve on the traditional terminology and objective consensus even more difficult than before.

In view of what we have seen it should hardly surprise us that the phenomenon of fanaticism can also be found as a pathological phenomenon in various groups of illnesses and that consequently it is often interpreted and classified in very diverse ways. Some authors, in their concentration on the conspicuous disturbance of affect in the fanatic, have counted him among the psychopathic fanatics or (especially in cases of mass-fanaticism) among the hysterics. But as soon as our judgment concerning fanatics concentrates more on their representation of values and of ideas the question urgently arises whether or not in some cases—above all in the historically important fanatics—they are prepsychotic personalities belonging to the schizoid group and whether or not one should speak of the severely compulsive character of some fanatics, since they are driven by compulsive ideas and compulsive tendencies.

In all these clinical classifications, however, we must keep in mind that the fanatics in question are not fanatic "because" they are psychopaths or hysterics, schizoids or compulsive individuals but that the clinical view merely intends to complete the picture of the fanatic thus far delineated without pretending to have causal explanations. Such explanations are not possible, for the clinical cases are almost always the "little" fanatics who play out their fanaticism without powerful conviction and generally also without sufficient vital energy within the family, a sect, or an association. (The "great" fanatics scarcely ever seek psychological treatment and also are not "committed.") Nevertheless these clinical observa-

tions are valuable since they bring clarity into the picture
of fanaticism and allow us to see specific traits which
have not yet come up for discussion in our context.

I. FANATICISM AS PSYCHOPATHY

1. THE CONCEPT OF PSYCHOPATHY

The terms "psychopathy" and "psychopathic" have
gradually been replaced in the last twenty or thirty years
by terms more in use in the scientific discussion of neurosis and psychosis. This is reasonable enough when we
consider that not only psychiatrists and psychologists
but educators, sociologists, politicians, and business exec-
utives make liberal application of the term "psychopathic." Nevertheless we cannot disregard the usefulness
of this term whenever it characterizes a kind of psychic
behavior and forms of reaction which seem quite clearly
different from our picture of neurosis and psychosis. Kurt
Schneider, whose book *Psychopathic Personalities* is still
quite topical, contests the assumption that "there are
no constitutional psychopaths."[2] In his definition of the
term "psychopath" he is in close agreement with Kraepelin, Birnbaum, Gruhle, Koch, Ziehen, and others, even
though a comparison of terms shows how extremely difficult it is to come to clear definitions in the psychological-
psychiatric realm.

For Schneider psychopathic personalities are "abnormal personalities who either suffer personally because of
their own abnormality or make the community suffer be-

cause of it."[3] Thus the abnormal personality is not sick but rather "a variation upon an accepted yet broadly conceived range of average personality." Schneider describes ten types of psychopathic personality. One of these is the fanatic psychopath who brings suffering on the community, the "disturbing psychopath," but "it should not be imagined that a psychopathic personality is just an asocial person, misfit, or criminal or in fact just anybody who annoys the community. This is to adopt a sociological or political definition of psychopathy which is wholly alien to the present approach. Psychopathic personalities are abnormal personalities who because of their personality anomaly readily come into conflict with life."[4] In another place he states even more clearly: "It is beyond any doubt that there is something constitutional in the psychopathic personality. . . . to regard that which we call disposition as the result of early childhood conflict and therefore so wish to understand it leads into an impenetrable darkness where only phantasy can shed light."[5]

This conception is very much in agreement with our own view of certain forms of fanaticism. It seems to us that certain fanatics must be seen as psychopaths, that they are, in fact, psychopathic because of their abnormal being-different—which basic difference can then, as secondary effect, be manifested as fanatic, or asocial, or even criminal behavior. To a great extent we can also follow Schneider in his description of the fanatic psychopath,

since this description is in accord with many of our own
expositions in the first and second chapter of this book.
But in saying this we must always keep in mind that only
certain types of fanatics are characterized as psychopaths
and that there are very many fanatics in whom other
clinical aspects are in the foreground.

2. CHARACTERISTICS OF FANATIC PSYCHOPATHY

In the fanatic psychopaths Schneider finds the traits of
querulousness and dogmatism especially prevalent. They
are (as J. L. Koch and E. Kraepelin agree) individuals
who are "unpleasantly insistent on their rights as liti-
gants and become strident for justice, carrying enough
conscience, as Koch remarked, for the whole world," and
they "adorn their embarrassment with a kind of public
importance, sometimes with a happy disregard for details."[6] "Koeppen noted that at the root of such developments we often find a real though not necessarily weighty
injustice. It is this that turns the man with a general
grouse into a singleminded fanatic. Kretschmer has
shown that such a conflict, especially when the individual
feels helpless against the forces of society, can lead to that
expansive development which he called combative paranoia where the typical carefree, healthy, expansive attitude is lost and the concentrated nursing of the thorn in
the flesh takes its place."[7]

Schneider, along with Birnbaum and Stertz, sees as
psychopaths also those fanatics who are conspicuous in

the oddity and eccentricity of their behavior and also in their thinking and striving: certain "nature-lovers," "true men," sectarians, such as the sanctimonious Saints of Königsberg, who in an extremely exaggerated and reality-hostile way disseminate ideas which, without doubt, can at times be quite valuable in themselves. Often enough there are also the mere "hangers-on" who seek their self-worth through a restless and fanatic dependency on a "führer"; adolescents who project their own conflicts with authority into social and political situations—which explains why almost all revolutionary movements try to win over the youth and especially the young intellectuals. There are also feminine hangers-on whose erotic relationships to prominent members of the movements often play an unconscious role.[8]

In this connection it is obvious that such anomalies cannot be called "illness," at least in the ordinary sense. "The term illness should be kept only for severe anomaly,"[9] but it is then difficult to draw an exact line between the healthy and sick. Moreover we should take note that only subnormal behavior is considered to be undesirable, detrimental and inferior, not that of the above average and the genius.

Therefore, insofar as fanaticism can be understood as psychopathy it is not a mental disease and should not be confused with feeble-mindedness or with schizoform or manic kinds of behavior. Several writers are much in accord that it is rather a *disturbance of affect*. Stertz emphasizes that "there is an increased affectivity and a peculiar splitting-proneness of the personality under the influence of the affects. In accordance with the instinctual drive of the latter and in accordance with the temperament, some become men of action and others may become silent martyrs for their conviction."[10] In referring to his own cases he says: "Whatever deviated from the norm, whatever was odd and even pathological lay in their constant and lively affect-accompaniment, which resulted in a noticeable overvaluation, lack of criticism, and incorrigibility, as well as a surprising lack of regard of the real situation. . . ."[11] Quite often they struggle for the same ideas and programs that are loudly argued by the general public at every get-together, but in the case of the fanatic they become supremely important and are defended with the urgency of a life and death situation.

The *cause* of such a disproportionate affect-accompaniment is seen by some writers in the dissonance of the psychic dispositions, in a disharmony which makes psychic equilibrium difficult. Such disharmonies seem to be constitutional, "inherent," and are generally observable during the entire life of the individual. Horstmann says: "The fanatic is in fact born with his strange psychic constitution; he *must* become a zealot, and, depending merely on the place and time in which he lives, he will fight with his whole person for Buddha, for Christ, Mohammed, Marx, or for General Booth."[12] Other writers, especially those from the school of depth psychology, put more emphasis on environmental influences and refer to a psychopathic development, which for them is equated with neurotic development.

Moreover we cannot disregard that the lack of moderation and the interior unconditionality by which psychopathic fanatics spare no expense and go to the very limit can be nourished also by sexual undercurrents made evident in an often conspicuous sadistic cruelty and masochistic self-humiliation. Then the dammed-up instincts are discharged in some type of disordinate affect-attitude for a relatively good idea or for some strange program. Some of these fanatic psychopaths are found in the ranks of confirmed bachelors, teetotalers, and vegetarians. Wilhelm Heinen has also dealt with this complex problem and comes to like conclusions:

"The sadistic-masochistic component in some forms of rigorism is, when carefully analyzed, unmistakable. What happened among some sects in the Middle Ages, for instance the Cathari, Waldensians, Flagellants, and in the fourteenth to seventeenth centuries with the trials of witches and heretics during the Inquisition and the Reformation in the name of pure doctrine and purged religion has been and is practiced in our century in the name of and for the protection of political orthodoxy and fidelity to the ideological line. The methods of torture and extortion employed by the servants of pseudo-religious cults in many shades of materialism, national socialism and bolshevism of whatever origin outdo the worst sadism of every religious inquisition. [Cf. Anton Böhm, *Epoche des Teufels* (Stuttgart, 1955).] Today it is no longer a secret that at all times and in all professions dealing directly with man (education, medicine, and the military) sadists have been at work and have borne fruit. Of all the forms of sadistic, masochistic and sadistic-masochistic reaction, the subtle, camouflaged forms, especially in the realm of religious-moral education, are the most difficult to diagnose. In rigorism they betray themselves rather obviously. Since both sadism and masochism are hidden and often unconscious sources of pleasure, the pleasure-drive of greedy love, so carefully avoided and devaluated by the rigorist, nevertheless comes to term, although by roundabout ways. The greedy appetite of the lower eros, often radically banished, is a secret cohabitant of the walled fortress from which the rigorist thunders and blasts. Whoever seeks to eliminate or to paralyze the efforts of the threefold drive will indirectly pay his toll, be it through perversions or through unsuccessful overcompensations."[13]

With essential exceptions, especially those emphasized by Kretschmer,[14] we can agree with Miller de la Fuente, who sees inner disharmony also as a "symptom of *inferiority*" whereby this inferiority is mainly the inability "to put oneself into the mentality and way of thinking of those who think differently and to recognize their equal rights—even if they are in error." The lack of restraint and the instinctuality resulting from this inability fit quite well into the general profile of the psychopathic fanatic.[15] In these cases it seems simply an overcompensation for inner deficiencies. These psychopathic fanatics seek to free themselves from their own feelings of inferiority by exaggerated self-confidence. But the inner split is indiscriminately transported to the outside as inordinate emotional passion for an idea or for a "führer" and, on the other side, as an inhuman callousness and sadistic cruelty toward "enemies."

We find examples of this in the reports of the trials of the commanders and assistants of the Nazi concentration camps. In one of the bills of indictment we read: "Neither parents nor upbringing, neither professional training nor education, not even a humanistic or academic education, neither religion nor family ties had the least influence on the criminal activity of the accused. None of them suffered a mental or physical breakdown. . . . even today they lack, in a kind of moral insanity, any feeling for the inexpressible misery they inflicted on numerous victims. . . . The armed SS played a decisive role in the Auschwitz murder machine. The high SS officials of the camp lacked every qualification of an officer. They knew neither a gentlemanly way of fighting nor fair treatment of the beaten enemy at their mercy and without defense. They were pitiful cowards and anything military was but ornamentation and imitation. The prosecutor said that even the myth of iron discipline and manly control was destroyed. On the contrary, licentiousness, larceny, profiteering in gold, venality, extreme corruption, and drunkenness were the order of the day in their ranks."[16]

After these illustrations it seems superfluous to emphasize that examples of such psychopathic fanatics—in the sense of a disturbed emotional functioning—can be found in every era and in every political, social, and religious totalitarianism. These "inferior" fanatics in the service of totalitarian systems have always existed. The very fact that inquisitions and witch trials were possible in the "Christian" centuries and that concentration camps and deportations can be actualized in our "socialized" era should make us very wary of our faith in the progress of technology, culture, and religion.

The picture of the psychopathic fanatic would be incomplete were we to disregard a third trait which is often coupled with the disturbance of the feeling-life and with inferiority symptoms, namely *life-alienation*. The inner unconditionality that knows no openness to communication and moderation does not adjust to life and people. The schemata of thinking are too narrow and immature. Among psychopathic fanatics, even among the older ones, we find surprisingly often the individual who has remained in some ways puerile and even infantile and who tries to force others into the Procrustean bed of his idealistic concepts. In Von Muralt's *Wahnsinniger oder Prophet?* the teacher, K. Huber, says: "The world must be full of love," and then he proceeds to disturb a public church service on a holyday in the belief that he has to unmask the "swindle."[17]

When today depth psychology time and again faces the problem of the adult who has remained on a childish level, the *puer aeternus,*[18] it sees in addition to psychic lability the life-alienation we have just spoken of. Such persons generally compensate for their naively uncritical infantilism with an inner counter-figure very much in contrast to the submissive, obedient, and very idealistic adolescent. We refer to this counter-figure as the "inner opponent," who, for example, as brutal father, inhuman dictator, criminal tyrant (or in the case of the *puella aeterna* as "strict mother," unnatural mother, *femme fatale*), both attracts and repels the adolescent but makes him an absolute follower of such a leader. Not infrequently such inner counter-authorities come to life some day in the external world if the opportunity offers itself. Then the victim of such complexes himself becomes a fanatic "führer" and recruits his own disciples (generally made up of adolescents and students). Almost all the radical movements of the last two decades could be investigated as to this scheme of development—and they would confirm it.

In concluding this section we need not emphasize that the "great" fanatics mentioned earlier cannot be seen simply from the viewpoint of psychopathy even though some of the peculiarities discussed here can also be found in them. But in our treatment many "little" fanatics are, from the clinical viewpoint, adequately characterized.

II. FANATICISM AS HYSTERIA

1. THE CONCEPT OF HYSTERIA

The term "hysteria" has also declined during the last few decades. But even more than in the case of the word "psychopathy" excessive use of the term "hysteria" in the clinical realm had degraded it into a vulgar invective. Nevertheless, we do have need of this term. It covers at least two characteristics that cannot easily be expressed with the term "neurosis." These two qualities are psychic lability and the hereby effected surrender to the reflector-psychic mechanism and to the well-known defense mechanisms of identification and projection. The two characteristics are closely interconnected. It is only because the psychic lability of some persons is so conspicuously great that they are so quickly at the mercy of reflector mechanisms or that they allow themselves, in a naive lack of criterion, to be driven by such mechanisms.

2. CHARACTERISTICS OF FANATIC HYSTERIA

Psychic lability is indicative of a disproportionally great lack of psychic equilibrium, a readiness to yield to momentary stimuli and impressions, and to extremes. It points to the absence of a self-secure center and of a core resting in itself. The development of a conscious, healthy ego has not taken place. Thus this ego is tossed back and forth between feelings of superiority and inferiority complexes. The lack of a relatively well-established ego simultaneously causes in these individuals the lack of a calm and healthy judgment, of a secure sense of value, and persevering determination. They are at the mercy of moods and tempers, and often they themselves are only too ready to yield to them. Whenever the personal core has remained so weak the well-known reflector mechanisms can exercise their control over the person. Such individuals are quickly gripped by the "storm of movement," and almost without transition the "feigned-death" reflex suddenly takes over, a silence and complete withdrawal, a paralysis and apathy.

Is not such a weak and almost necessarily constantly fluctuating psychic condition a far cry from the fanatic attitude which presupposes never letting go of an idea once it is grasped as valuable? In fact, important, "great" fanatics can hardly be considered as mere hysterics. Yet hysteric traits can very well be seen in combination with the fanatic attitude, and we often find them also in fanatics. Especially when it is less a matter of fanatic endurance than of fanatic outbreaks, the reflector mechanism can play an important role. It is a well-known fact that fanatics can at times exercise a mysterious fascination. They put the public into raving ecstasies, orgies of enthusiasm or indignation. Such power of fascination can hardly be comprehended without consideration of the unrestraint and intensity of the hysteric mechanism. In

such moments some fanatics give themselves up completely to their blind instincts and awaken the same
instincts in the masses. It is above all this hysteric component which sets off fanatic explosions of masses and of
young people. Hysterical behavior is almost always con-
tagious, especially for a mass or crowd, in which, as we
know, the individual sense of responsibility is reduced
so that on the lower psychic level the reflector mechanism
can break out uncontrolled. Everything that has had
to be dammed up and kept down in everyday life, the
longing for a freer and less burdensome life but also
instincts of revenge against other classes and statuses can
be unleashed. Therefore great masses are often the victim
of a fanatic movement, the fascinating orator, the "drum-
beater" rather than having in themselves the power to
organize and carry through fanatic movements. They are
the will-less but inexpendable instruments of the fanatic
leader.

In fanaticism not only the reflex mechanisms are at
work but the unconscious psychic mechanisms of *identification* and *projection* are also stirred into action. In a
fanaticized mob an unconscious mechanic identification
with its instigators and their slogans takes place, and
with equal suddenness projection raises its head and
accuses the enemy of corruption, gluttony, degeneracy—
all the accusations which have remained strangely stereotyped during the centuries. It can create real psychic
infections, like pathological epidemics, in entire com-

munities and groups of nations. We may recall here our description of the convulsionaries of 1731–1732.[19]

It is even more disgusting when such identifications and projections lead to horrible fanatic excesses and finally become a means of public amusement. H. C. Lea writes at length about the expensive preparations of an auto-da-fé (the condemnation and burning of heretics) in the seventeenth and even at the beginning of the eighteenth century in Spain: "A writer, in 1724, giving an account of the autos celebrated in Seville since 1719, is vastly more concerned with enumerating the names of officials and familiars, with describing the ceremonial and dilating upon the crimson velvet chairs and cushions and canopies embroidered in gold and silver and the diamond badges worn by the functionaries, than with the real work of the tribunal, grim and cruel though it continued to be. . . . When the Spaniard regarded it [the auto-da-fé] as a celebration fitted for a day of rejoicing, or as a spectacular entertainment acceptable to distinguished national guests, he did so in the conviction that it was the highest exhibition of piety, and a service to God, glorious to the land which organized it, and stimulating the devotion of all participants. . . . The great auto of Madrid, in 1632, was held there by the special order of the king, in celebration of the recovery from confinement of Isabelle de Bourbon, wife of Philip IV, and was graced with the presence of both and of their son Don Carlos."[20]

Inasmuch as hysterical traits are strongly combined with fanatic behavior there arises almost necessarily the suspicion of psychic *inauthenticity*. Working oneself into highest degrees of excitement or even allowing oneself to be passively swept up by it becomes at a certain moment a half-unconscious untruth and a lie. The caricaturing of the enemy, the black and white description of a social or political situation, the inordinate demands show that it is no longer a matter of justice, of true freedom for all, and of a natural order but of an instinct-driven showing off, an egotistical self-superiority and thus a basis of profound inner untruthfulness.

For example let us test our feelings about Hitler's self-justification which he made before a small group on September 1, 1939, after he had declared war on Poland. Dahlerus gives us this account: "He grew more and more excited, and began to wave his arms as he shouted in my face: 'If England wants to fight for a year, I shall fight for a year; if England wants to fight two years, I shall fight two years. . . .' He paused and then yelled, his voice rising to a shrill scream and his arms milling wildly: 'If England wants to fight for three years, I shall fight for three years. . . .' The movements of his body now began to follow those of his arms, and when he finally bellowed: 'Und wenn es erforderlich ist, will ich zehn Jahre Kämpfen' [And, if necessary, I will fight for ten years], he brandished his fist and bent down so that it nearly touched the floor. The situation was highly embarrassing, so embarrassing in fact that Göring reacted perceptibly to the spectacle Hitler was making of himself by turning on his heel so that he had his back to both of us."[21]

It need not be especially stressed that the example of Hitler shows very clearly the role hysteria can play in fanaticism. Furthermore, when we think how much in Hitler fanaticism also played a conscious role and was employed as a means and how much he incited fanaticism in others, we cannot fail to see the strange psychic ambivalence which manifests itself in the fact that the outbreaks of such fanatics generally originate in an injured self-confidence and simultaneously give rise to a narcissistic self-gratification and are thus an ever new temptation. The hysterical mechanism of the storm of movement and the feigned-death reflex provide the fanatic with excellent means of producing external effects and of blackmailing his enemies—and, at the same time, of experiencing self-gratification in the unleashing of peak intensities of emotion.

III. FANATICISM IN THE SCHIZOID SYNDROME

The schizoid syndrome comprises quite a number of symptoms which by no means can be called psychotic in the strict sense. Thus these symptoms do not simply foretell the eventual eruption of a schizophrenic episode. At times, however, they may be in evidence before such an outbreak so that subsequently they can be interpreted

as "prepsychotic." Yet they may also remain in the
strange halfway state between illness and health and
can decisively co-determine the psychic situation for a
lifetime.

1. THE PSYCHIC RIGIDITY OF THE IDEATION PROCESS

There are especially three typical behaviors which
must be seen as such symptoms in the context of the
problem of fanaticism. What first strikes one is the psychic rigidity of thinking and ideation in respect to the
appropriate contents. The very same images, associations,
and ideas almost literally capture such an individual,
possess him without his being capable of dealing and
coping with them in a realistic, objective way. He is
"obsessed" by them and not infrequently wants to force
others into the same obsession. Such a rigid process of
psychic functioning necessarily implies the fixation of
psychic energy on a very few points or even on a single
point of the psychic "energy field." Not only is the one
thing emphasized but this one thing is the only thing
perceived out of the multiplicity and entirety of possibilities; it alone is heard in every conversation and in
every speech, is read in every book and article and becomes ever more fixated. "I will only love," "my happi-
ness is love," is the stereotyped repetition of teacher
Huber, who disturbed the Sunday service.[22] For such
persons there is only one possible life-attitude, only one
subject of conversation around which their psychic life

rotates, only one legitimate form of government, only one approach to art that is truly creative. Therefore such individuals almost by necessity become integralists and advocate absolute control and totalitarianism in all areas in which they are active. "Every experience is sifted, so to speak, through the sieve of 'faith' before any position is taken," says Kujath, who clearly recognized this rigidity and fixation in some of his patients and put it on record in the case of H. as follows:

"H. is a pale, asthenic, blond, middle-aged man; his facial expression is rigid, his tone monotonous, his manner of speaking ponderous, in the style of the Old Testament. He and German grammar don't get along. His attitude is that of one lost to the world. There is something martyrish, resigned and at the same time stubborn and accusing reflected in his physiognomy with its wide-open, fixated eyes and almost masklike, immobile features. When his ideas are challenged a pitiful, self-complacent smile plays around the corners of his mouth, but it soon fades away into his impenetrable mask. When questioned he answers from the start with a full repertoire of biblical quotations. At first it seems impossible to get him to speak of his own experiences or to take a stand. H. is always anxious to evade the situation with clichés and the insistence that he has distanced himself from everything personal. But as rapport increases in the course of conversation one gets the impression that here one is dealing with a very definite attitude that is the result of his mentality: for almost every thought the appropriate biblical quotation is sought."[23]

Kretschmer, too, recognizes these viscous and blocked-up courses of thinking and ideation in schizoids. Along with Bleuler he speaks of "affect-rigidity" when trying to characterize the psycho-motility of the schizoids. With this Kretschmer discovers even further peculiarities as part of such a rigid style of functioning: parallelism, rhythmizing, stereotypy and symmetry in the entire behavior and expression.[24]

Pfahler, in a similar though somewhat weaker way—because of his distinctive conception of fanaticism mentioned earlier—insists that the disposition to fanatic behavior is found only in the type groups with "persistent, tenacious, and limited attention," which by nature lack motility, modulation-capacity and psychic elasticity. His opinion is in turn confirmed by Kujath's investigation. Concerning the above-mentioned case of H. Kujath writes:

"According to Pfahler the examination of personality types employing the word-series test in which the subject is instructed to arrange several successively presented words into a given theme on his own (for example, feast of harvest) shows an essential tendency to cling tenaciously to the initial idea, a fact which is strikingly evident when inappropriate words are deliberately given intending to distract the attention from the theme. The elaboration of thought is poor in ideas and in general a textbook description is presented. The sentence formation is awkward. The sequence of ideas remains within the nearest at hand. The same results are found from the Rorschach test. The number of given interpretations is small, form-critical comments predominate. Other tests, too, indicate a narrow, fixated way of thinking with a strong sense of responsibility for correct interpretation. This makes it clear that in the case of H. we deal with a definite type of fixed contents. According to the original Rorschach method H. is of a predominantly reproductive intelligence with pedantic, stereotyped, and affect-suppressing tendencies. Alongside a lack of extratension we find a rigid, stabilized affectivity. The entire attitude suggests passivity and resignation. The presentation of incomplete stimuli (O. Müller) indicates, in the clinging to particular details of the exposed aggregates, in the lack of phantasy, the dislike of symbolism and finally, in the weak tendency toward meaningful synthesis, the characteristics of a predominantly disintegrated type as defined by Jaensch."[25]

Even the fanatics of a "new freedom" and a "true tolerance" manifest the same inflexible, inelastic attitude. Their fight is always for the freedom "which *I* mean," and they suppress that of the others the moment they take control of a nation or community or gain a position of authority in the public eye. All too often today's hero of freedom is tomorrow's brutal dictator. World history still attests to this fact even today. The fact is that the rigid attitude is not caused by the ideal fought for but by the psychic makeup of the particular function-structure. Lenin "liked to employ constantly and ever more emphatically the one same formula which seemed suitable to direct the attention of his audience to an important point." Trotsky once said: "Lenin always sings the same song, that of the need to radically change the social differences among men." And Woronski, the Bolshevik critic, says that Lenin talks only on the one same theme: "He views the same statement from the most diverse and unexpected sides, often ten times. He speaks like a man who has always the same idea, the idea of ideas, around which the fragments of all other thoughts rotate like planets around the sun."[26]

How closely joined are the extremes of hysterical lability and exaggerated unrest on the one hand and monomanic rigidity and complete intransigence on the other is uniquely demonstrated in another dictator of our century: Hitler. From 1913 to 1945 Hitler stubbornly held on to his central and basic dogma concerning international Jewry. A thorough reading of his two-volume *Mein Kampf* shows that by 1913 Hitler's attitude toward the Jews as individuals and as a "race" was set once and for all and as a basic dogma determined all his other concepts of politics, economics, art, and science. Time and again he described the Jew as an "element of decomposition" in all areas of culture, as decaying, dissolving, and poisoning. The impressions Hitler acquired in Vienna in

his early years made him see the Jew not only as the
enemy of the German nation but as the worst destroyer
of all human values. The strong representation of Jews
in science (especially in medicine) and also in art was an
abomination to him. Bullock says:

"Just as Hitler ascribed to the 'Aryan' all the qualities
and achievements which he admired, so all that he hated
is embodied in another mythological figure, that of the
Jew. There can be little doubt that Hitler believed what
he said about the Jews; from first to last his anti-Semitism
is one of the most consistent themes in his career, the master idea which embraces the whole span of his thought.
In whatever direction one follows Hitler's train of
thought, sooner or later one encounters the satanic figure
of the Jew. The Jew is made the universal scapegoat.
Democracy is Jewish—the secret domination of the Jew.
Bolshevism and Social Democracy; capitalism and the
'interest-slavery' of the moneylender; parliamentarianism
and the freedom of the Press; liberalism and internation-
alism; anti-militarism and the class war; Christianity;
modernism in art (*Kultur-Bolschewismus*), prostitution
and miscegenation—all are instruments devised by the
Jew to subdue the Aryan peoples to his rule. . . .

" 'The Jew has never founded any civilization, though
he has destroyed hundreds. He possesses nothing of his
own creation to which he can point. Everything he has is
stolen. Foreign peoples, foreign workmen build him his
temples; it is foreigners who create and work for him;

it is foreigners who shed their blood for him. He has no art of his own; bit by bit he has stolen it all from other peoples. He does not even know how to preserve the precious things others have created. . . . In the last resort it is the Aryan alone who can form States and set them on their path to future greatness. All this the Jew cannot do. And because he cannot do it, therefore all his revolutions must be international. They must spread as a pestilence spreads. Already he has destroyed Russia; now it is the turn of Germany, and with his envious instinct for destruction he seeks to disintegrate the national spirit of the Germans and to pollute their blood' (Speech at Munich, 28 July, 1922)."[27]

It is surprising with what unassailable naiveté this "Führer" of a great and cultured nation stuck to his fixed idea. When the war was lost and Hitler had decided upon his suicide in the bunker of the chancellery in Berlin he composed his political testament to the German people on April 29, 1945. This little-known document once more explicitly confirms the fact that Hitler's fight against the Jews was a *fanum,* something sacred, the reason only a fanatic effort would be enough to fulfill his bequest:

"It is untrue that I, or anyone else in Germany, wanted the war in 1939. It was desired and instigated solely by those international statesmen who were either of Jewish descent or worked for Jewish interests. . . . Centuries will pass away, but out of the ruins of our towns and monuments hatred will grow against those finally respon-

sible for everything, International Jewry, and its helpers.
. . . Above all I charge the leaders of the nation and
those under them to scrupulous observance of the laws
of race and to merciless opposition to the universal poi-
soner of all peoples, international Jewry."[28]

Concerning this testament Bullock wisely comments:

"Word for word, Hitler's final address to the German
nation could be taken from almost any of his early
speeches of the 1920s or from the pages of *Mein Kampf*.
Twenty-odd years had changed and taught him nothing.
His mind remained as tightly closed as it had been on
the day when he wrote: 'During these years in Vienna a
view of life and a definite outlook on the world took
shape in my mind. These became the granite basis of
my conduct. Since then I have extended that foundation
very little, I have changed nothing in it' (*Mein Kampf,*
p. 20)."[29]

For persons whose processes of thought and ideation
work in such a monomanic way this psychic immobility
is considered something especially valuable and is called
"inner strength," "steadfastness," and "fidelity," whereas
the more flexible type is seen as inconsistent, inferior,
and without character. This also explains their armored
intransigence. Any somewhat more objective approach
is considered suspicious and dangerous and is for these
individuals unrealizable and impossible. For this type
it is a psychic necessity to take a radical position in
every situation, which, although at times it may be seen

as a prosthesis for a labile condition, is in most cases a structure-given attitude.

2. IDENTIFICATION WITH THE IDEA

The rigid behavior of this type of fanatic generally builds up to a complete *identification* with the idea he advocates. With this we arrive at the second symptom pointing to the schizoid syndrome. Even though the processes of identification, like the processes of projection, belong to the universally human and therefore necessary mechanisms, depth psychology clearly recognizes those inadequate identifications which as defense mechanisms alienate man from his real identity and his innermost self and thus drive him into neurosis or the unfolding of a latent psychosis. It is a mysterious paradox in the rigid fanatic that his all too personal attitude suddenly turns into the apersonal zone of an alienating and inordinate identification. For in him the ego must not only take a stand for a cause and represent it with the entire person but it becomes swallowed up by this cause and as free person is hollowed out, gradually losing its human substantiality. It becomes, so to speak, the puppet of a foreign power, to which it is perforce inextricably chained, for better or for worse, "to the bitter end." It is the special peril of permanent identifications and overidentifications that the real ego shrinks more and more and is gradually replaced by phantastic, naive, or paranoid forms of identification.[30]

We have already mentioned the sweeping identifications of Savonarola, and Kujath's H. says: "My thoughts
are God's thoughts." Equally typical are fanatic identifications with the State and nation. Even if we do not wish
to adjudge Louis XIV fanatic, the statement ascribed to
him, "L'etat c'est moi," must at least make us think. This
statement, as we know, was taken over literally as the
slogan of the Nazi era: "Hitler is Germany and Germany
is Hitler." Every German enemy of the "Führer" became
automatically the enemy of his people and his country.
Such extreme identifications can no longer be considered
harmless and normal and their intransigent character leads
dangerously close to collective neuroses and psychoses.

Now, however, we come to the problematic point
where psychological categories seem too one-sided, since
overlapping relationships, social, metaphysical and religious attitudes come into play which in the individual
instance demand the taking of an ultimate stand. Who
would see the Buddhist monks who burned themselves
to death in Saigon in 1963 only as victims of an identification tendency, for instance a desire to return "into the
solitude of the womb of the great mother"? Or another
example: is it merely an unconscious, intrapsychic compensation mechanism when one is ready to die for his
country or his religion? Is suicide out of political, social,
religious protest always the result of a sick psyche? Does
the following report from Madras on February 12, 1965,
still belong in the context of the pathology of fanaticism

or does it belong in the book of heroic patriotism: "In protest against the introduction of Hindi as the vernacular, the director of the grade school of the village of the State of Madras poured benzine over himself and burned himself alive: This has been the fourth case of suicide by burning since the publication of the decree."[31] Every ideology has its prophets "who are stoned," martyrs who happily die for their truth. But on the other hand we should not forget the wars of religion (for instance, the massacre of the Albigensians) in which, on both sides, Christians tortured and killed one another for the sake of Christianity. Is it God-willed that men kill themselves for the sake of God?

At times the distinguishing criterion between fidelity to one's religion and fanaticism is certainly difficult to come upon. Generally, however, it is found in the fact that the rigid fanatic does not merely passively endure with an inner willingness but himself becomes aggressive, using terror, force and violence of the most horrible kind and perhaps even forms them into a system for the annihilation and liquidation of all opponents. He starts the attack against the "evil" and persecutes it with an ineradicable hatred. That with it the dormant yet waiting instincts of violence awaken is an ever newly observed fact. (The counsel "do not forcibly resist evil" has time and again been forgotten—repressed in the course of the centuries.)

Even when it does not lead to such extremes one thing

is always noticeable: *reaction to resistance*. The rigid fanatic cannot respond to resistance with yielding discussion or compromise. This way is closed to him. His only alternatives are to lose or to fight all the harder. The monomanic fanatic is incited by resistance. His answer then becomes: "Now let us start in earnest." The war becomes forthwith a "holy" war and the enemy is declared subhuman. How many fanatics have been stimulated by protests is worthy of consideration. Written protests cause fanatics to accelerate their effort. Carl Jakob Burckhardt, who was commissar of the League of Nations in Danzig previous to World War II, says concerning his efforts to save the Jews in Danzig: "In the course of the . . . tension-laden attempts to save the Jews of Danzig I was perfectly convinced that I had to avoid one thing: protest. Every protest immediately caused Hitler to resort to the most brutal measures."[32]

3. A FORM OF PARANOID DELUSION?

The psychic rigidity in the process of thought and ideation as well as ever increasing identification with the ideas and values striven for leads us to ask whether this cannot at times be a *form of paranoid delusion*.

It should make us pause and consider when most authors who deal with the problem voice this question. Kujath admits that "it seems at least debatable whether it is justified to place the fanatically defended, overvalued idea system on a parallel with rudimentary delusion."[33]

Stertz goes a step further and sees a clear "connection with those having a paranoid disposition." He points emphatically to the "danger of a paranoid development" in one of his cases. Although he says that none of the six cases treated by him were mentally ill, he nevertheless maintains: "Schizophrenic processes can occasionally be vested in a similar garb. In such instances it is to be expected that the defended ideas even content-wise gradually take on an eccentric and incoherent character."[34] And Horstmann writes: "It is not always possible to mark off the borderline where fanaticism ends and delusion begins."[35]

It is a fact that in most fanatics we observe exaggerations, simplifications, generalizations, one-sided interpretations, and even misinterpretations of their opponents' opinions, so that we speak with some justification of an "autistic," "dereistic" way of thinking, and at least the impression of an existing delusional system can be given. However, this is generally not a delusion in the sense of a perceptual delusion characteristic of psychotic schizophrenia but rather a "battle paranoia," which, due to emotional overheating in combination with rigidity and identification, is carried away by allegations and interpretations into suspicions and interpolations no longer corresponding to reality. Kurt Schneider has strikingly described this state of affairs:

"In our view delusion-formation has nothing to do

with traits of personality and there are serious objections to attempts which endeavour to associate the two. Delusion cannot be explained away in terms of a particular personality, its development and inner conflicts. Certain paranoid developments in primitive, sensitive, expansive and some atypical personalities may be taken as reactions to experience, but delusion proper and delusional perception when they appear do not belong to the sphere of abnormal personality at all nor to that of abnormal reaction any more than any other schizophrenic symptom does. The state is one of psychotic paraphrenia. The actual course of development cannot be traced through the delusional content but, as with all psychic contents, may be clarified in the light of the personality and its previous history. . . ." "Eccentrics of this sort often are or have been schizophrenic, and as Peratti showed they may well provide a rallying point round which other eccentric psychopaths gather."[36]

Even though it would be incorrect to put the fanatic in the psychotic category, the affinity with the schizoid syndrome cannot be ignored. It is so obvious that it at least deserves mention. Kretschmer with his constitutional typology has convincingly demonstrated that all important fanatics bear even in their bodily structure the characteristics of the schizothymic-schizoid syndrome: asthenic-leptosome, the angular profile, muscular rigidity, and so forth.[37]

IV. FANATICISM AS COMPULSION-PHENOMENON

1. THE NOTION OF COMPULSION

In the course of these discussions it has often been intimated that the fanatic is under a strong inner pressure. He is compelled to act. A foreign power seems to call him and force him into its service. Quite often it can even happen that the fanatic is not only willing to follow such a "call" but is happy and enthused about his "mission." The history of politics, of social life, of art and religion time and again gives accounts of persons who out of a great inner "obligation" became fanatic fighters for new ideas and programs. At times such a pressure condenses that there is a sense of actually being forced, of an inability to escape. In especially pronounced cases of this kind the Middle Ages spoke of "incubus," of a possession by "powers," by angels, or devils.

Depth psychology sees in these phenomena a psychic compulsion. In the therapy of neurosis it meets many forms of compulsive manifestations and it tries to determine their etiology. Here again arguments about the always imperfect terms are unavoidable. Many writers shy away from speaking about compulsive neuroses and try to avoid an exact labeling by using expressions such as "compulsive thoughts," "compulsive ideas," "compulsive drives" and "compulsive actions." For various reasons we shall just as warily speak only of "compulsive manifestations," which can be joined to our before-mentioned abnormal background of fanatic behavior so that fanaticism in our view is by no means to be understood merely as "compulsive neurosis" but reveals its character even more clearly as a resultant property of manifold and very complicated psychic border-states. Most pathologically compulsive individuals experience the compulsion (the idea, thought, feeling, impulse) as something imposed and forced upon them and its content generally appears as something absurd, so that they themselves feel as if possessed by compulsion. But the fanatic accepts and inwardly acknowledges the compulsion and at times fiercely approves of it. Even though felt as a force it is at the same time assimilated and integrated as being meaningful and value-enhancing. Therefore the compulsion of the fanatic must be clearly distinguished from that of the other compulsive types. This is also the reason the fanatic does not seek therapy and will angrily refuse it while other victims of compulsion wish to be cured. Some writers therefore refer to the compulsion of the fanatic as an "insession," in contradistinction to the obsession" of other pathological compulsives.[38]

2. CHARACTERISTICS OF FANATIC COMPULSION

The concrete manifestation of the fanatic compulsive attitude is determined by four distinguishing characteristics. First there is the character of the *inner force,* of the obligation which is extremely strong. The ideas and thoughts coming to the fore are not connected with the previous ego-person. Their foreignness and the intensity of their forceful entry are alarming. One cannot resist them but against his own will is at their mercy. Savonarola in one of his last sermons, on March 18, 1498, says that at home he had made the firm resolution: "From now on I will no longer speak and preach about these things but will be silent and let God work." And he goes on: "But then as soon as I am again on the pulpit I can no longer control myself. It becomes like fire burning in my heart (Jer. 20:9), I cannot do otherwise: I must speak; I feel myself full of fire and inflamed by the Lord. Back at home I again resolve: I will no longer speak about these things; and yet as soon as I am once more on the pulpit I cannot control my tongue and keep these words in check.[39]

Calvin experienced a similar compulsion: " 'Although my goal was always to live as a private individual without being famous, God so led me and through many vicissitudes spun me round as in a whirlwind that I could nowhere and never find peace until he put me, against my nature, in the limelight and caused me to go into action.' " "Even till the day of his death he [Calvin] said; that he 'always followed his call like one forced.' He feels like Jonas who must preach and teach against his will."[40] Such compulsion need not be discharged only in words; especially on the lower level of the demagogues it manifests ifself much more clearly in their expressive movements, their distorted gestures and in their tone.

Here again it is enough to recall Hitler's tense posture, his compulsive gestures, and the bellowing tone of his speeches. Listening to these hour-long eruptions one had the impression that he spoke not out of a calm and sensible judgment but out of a cramped condition that was both tormenting and tormentingly pleasurable. After all, Hitler did not appeal to the reason of his audience but moved heaven and earth to electrify and anesthetize his listeners.

This clearly recognizable compulsion is inwardly affirmed by the fanatic. The force is accepted as *"mission"* and fulfilled as "task." Not infrequently this mission is perceived as an internal or even external "voice" which conveys the "order." From such a power the "called" cannot escape.

Schnitzer writes concerning Savonarola: "It was tremendously impressive that Hieronymus drew upon a higher being for his predictions and referred to his clearly divine mission to guilt-laden mankind." "Whoever does not believe him cannot be a good Christian for he errs as little as God errs." Or another time: " 'Lord, if I act not out of the fullest conviction or if my words do not come from you then crush me in this very moment.' "[41] Pastor speaks of a "certain susceptibility of Savonarola for hallucinatory manifestations and states."[42] Often this "higher knowing" is connected with the sense of being chosen and called. Calvin also alludes to such a call: "Since in my conscience I was convinced that what I have

thought and written by no means grew from my brain
but that I received it from *God,* I must adhere to it would
I not be traitor to the truth."[43]

It may seem incomprehensible in this context, yet psychologically we cannot throw it aside, that even a Hitler
believed he had to refer to a higher power. Was it merely
an act of hysterical ostentation or skillful calculation
bordering on blasphemy, or was it an actual inner compulsion when after his march into Vienna he culminated
a speech with the following statements: "In three days
the Lord has smitten them. . . . And to me the grace was
given on the day of the betrayal to be able to unite my
homeland with the Reich. . . . I would now give thanks
to Him who let me return to my homeland in order that
I might now lead it into my German Reich. Tomorrow,
may every German recognize the hour, and measure its
import and bow in humility before the Almighty who in
a few weeks has wrought a miracle upon us."[44]

Hearing these words from the mouth of one who with
clever calculation has worked his "miracle" by violence
and broken treaties could make our hair stand on end.
And yet we have to see Hitler as a severely pathological
person in whom inner contradictions ran riot, sweeping
him from sentimentalities to cold-blooded acts of terror
and finally to the unscrupulous slaughtering of millions
of people.

Not only those fanatics who play a codetermining
role in world history allude to higher inspirations or
even hear "voices"; also less significant fanatics some-

times maintain that they hear such "voices." Von Muralt reports that his patient, the teacher Huber, said even in his early youth: "It is always as though a voice in me says that I am destined for something great." "I also feel every day more clearly that God has destined me to something great and I put myself self-sacrificingly into his service." "The voice says: 'you must'—and I answer: 'I will.' " This created in him an ecstatic feeling of joy.[45]

A third characteristic in the fanatic compulsive is the *fixation tendency* of his thoughts and ideas. What we noticed in the schizoid syndrome as "rigidity in the process of thought and ideation" we also find here, but it is condensed into compulsive behavior. The compulsive fanatic is committed to an exactly fixed wording and fidelity to the letter. His ideas and thoughts are always vested in the very same formula. Thus even his way of speaking takes on something of the character of a formula. With an almost deliberate monotone he creates a hypnotic effect. These individuals seem to believe that the great and essential, the incomprehensible and mysterious can be captured in a single magic formula. This compulsion for a ready-made and final formula necessarily degenerates into a repetition compulsion in which the overwhelmed ego experiences over and over the magic power of the formula. Whole communities can assimilate such stereotyped formulas, which develop into a distinctive jargon creating a close unity among the "initiated."

We have already referred to the stereotyped phrases

of Lenin. Hitler's style, too, shows the same peculiar stereotype. Of course, here we no longer deal with a completely "unconscious" compulsion, since repetition is also applied as a very conscious rhetorical method and demagogical manner of speaking. Yet it can hardly be avoided that the constant hammering-in not only of the same thought but also of the solidly set formula has a retroactive effect on the speaker. With every repetition he once more inwardly compels himself not so much in order to convince or persuade his listeners but to compel them too. This force gradually becomes so intense that the entire way of life of the compulsive fanatic is narrowed down and withdrawn from other influences. The experience of analysis teaches us how much repetition compulsion is at the core of the neurotic processes.[46] Hence the compulsive fanatic lives in "his" world, a world that more and more loses contact with the real world. It is reported that in the last three years of the war Hitler refused to visit any of the bombed cities (with the exception of Berlin), just as "he refused to read reports which contradicted the picture he wanted to form."[47] "He was fighting for something more than his power or his skin; he was fighting to preserve intact that image he had created of himself as one of Hegel's 'World Historical Individuals.' "[48] Hitler had himself become a victim of Hitlerism.

In regard to these compulsive fanatics one cannot but think of Karl Spitteler's striking formulation: "*Ananke,* the compelled compulsion." Once again we must go back chiefly to the ethical form-fanaticism and to all forms of rigorism. The problem of the "scrupulous" must in most cases be seen from this viewpoint of compulsive phenomena, even when one deals with the "colorless" fanatics who generally do not in the least want to hurt anyone else but who consequently all the more radically torment themselves. In fact, the "anankasts" are the fanatics who reach the highest degree of inner un-freedom.

Finally we must emphasize a fourth characteristic of the compulsive fanatic: *aggression*. Aggression can be clearly seen in most fanatic compulsive types ranging from relatively harmless ridicule and sarcasm on to the more serious form of quarrelsomeness and chicanery and finally ending up with excessive cruelty and deliberately devised torture. It is frightening and alarming when even religious and pious fanatics manifest merciless and cruel aggression. We have to admit that even Savonarola and Calvin were not free of these unchristian tendencies. Quite early in his life Savonarola thundered against gambling with the words: "Cursed be all who gamble or allow gambling," "they are the servants of the devil,"[49] and during the final year of his life it was a matter of course for him to call his enemies nothing but "godless people and devils."[50] Calvin was not only very rude but expressed a presumptuous and unchristian aggression against all enemies of his kingdom of God. His dictatorial rule of even the most detailed daily affairs of his family life was already conspicuous enough, but Calvin's true face showed through most clearly when he demanded much more insistently than the Council of Geneva that "more witches be found and burned."[51] Thomas Müntzer was convinced that God had entrusted him with the vocation of a "destroyer of unbelievers" and the "sword of Gideon," and hence he concluded that he was "not to spare anyone who resists the word of God."[52]

But revolutionaries and politicians who are less Christian can display the same radically merciless behavior. The French Revolution strove with blood and terror for its ideal of freedom. Carrier, a deputy of the National Convention, stated coldly: "We would rather turn France into a graveyard than give up ruling it in our way."[53] One hundred and fifty years later, however, we find the very same type in Baretzki, of the Auschwitz concentration camp, about whom the public prosecutor said: "He tortured and murdered on his own initiative and assiduously pursued tasks which were beyond the orders given to him in his striving to excel. In his SS uniform the little corporal felt like a superman to whom Jews, Poles, and Russians were only 'subhumans' without the right to live. In so doing he attained the lowest level of disreputable mental attitude."[54]

3. BACKGROUNDS OF FANATIC COMPULSION

To illumine the *backgrounds* of the phenomenon of fanatic compulsion with its peculiar sadistic-masochistic component is one of the most difficult tasks facing psychiatry, brain pathology, general physiological pathology, and especially depth psychology. When we limit ourselves to a purely psychic view of the genesis of the compulsive syndrome, disregarding the fact that physiological changes of the organism as a whole—brain tumors, for instance—can also evoke such a syndrome, we must above all take into account two psychodynamic attempts at explanation: Sigmund Freud's theory of repression and C. G. Jung's theory of the invasion of archaic ideas and impulses out of the collective unconscious.

Aggressive, sadistic compulsive behavior is hardly explainable without the participation of repressed tendencies that have been pushed into the unconscious. The repressed primary pleasure instinct seeks to force through its satisfaction by the side-channels of sadistic-masochistic impulses. Quite obviously then this is no longer a spontaneous victory of pleasure resulting from original vitality and its overactivity. In the overflow of energy manifested in the true hyperthymic[55] we observe neither the compulsive element nor the urge to torture. The gratification of the sadistic compulsive fanatic, however, is a secondary, reactive pleasure resulting from the explosion of long dammed-up or inadequately fulfilled primary instincts. It is a deeply interior, secret satisfaction which the fanatic experiences in such outbreaks, even though it can be simultaneously equally unpleasant. This very ambivalence of a simultaneous sense of pleasure and displeasure makes it quite clear that it is not a matter of natural pleasure based on an enhanced and meaningful vitality but of a subsequent and compensatorily achieved in-spite-of satisfaction of stored-up and restless, too long "frustrated" and cheated instinctual needs.

The more violent and long-lasting the damming up of primary impulses the more vehement are the discharges. Often these discharges occur without a clearly recognizable motive; at a certain instance they are simply "due" and strike the fanatic himself and, of course, his environment with elemental force. But instead of such periodical discharges a permanent aggressive attitude can also develop, a constant readiness to spring and unflagging irritation. Kunz wisely observes that this reactive aggression does not experience the autonomous change of phases of tension and relaxation, of restlessness and restfulness, of need and fulfillment as do the spontaneous instincts but that there exists an erratic readiness to spring or a permanent readiness for aggression.[56] An appropriate analogy to the individual permanent attitude of aggression is seen in the permanent purges which almost every totalitarian system with its secret police is forced to carry out: every force necessarily provokes the counterforce; no human activity escapes this law.

A special form of the aggressive compulsive attitude is found in the "counterposition." It manifests itself as a picayunishly exact, pedantic, and hence tormenting form of opposition to the instinctual aggression compulsion. For instance, we meet the fanatics of excessive cleanliness

who overcompensate for their delight in filth, or the scrupulous who torment themselves with unrelenting pangs
of conscience since they know only too well how con-
scienceless they can be the moment they repress their
scruples. The rigorist rightly fears his inner laxism.

But the repression mechanism as disclosed by Freud
reveals several aspects which permit a deeper understanding of fanaticism as a tormenting-gratifying compulsion phenomenon. We can speak of an almost desperate
and hence symptomatically compulsive attempted breakthrough of energies too long imprisoned. Fanatic compulsive behavior can cause an individual with a somewhat
childish fixation to think that he is leaving a labile,
dangerous psychic situation and entering a world of
established, objective, and even absolute order. It is clear
that such attempted breakouts can strive for various
object-worlds: it depends upon disposition and the situation in time whether one seeks reputation in the technological, athletic, political, social, artistic, scientific, or
religious realm. One can also speak of the unconscious
anxiety defense of an inflated and hence insecure super-
ego which, in a mustering up of an ultimate force of
compulsion, must constantly repress the inevitable depressions and irritations into the unconscious-anony-
mous id and thus sadistic-masochistic behavior is almost
unavoidable. Finally we can fix our gaze on the fanatic's
narcissistic *self-gratification* during his tortured orgies
and see the flame of libidinal satisfaction burning in the

midst of compulsion and at the center of his cruel destructive activity. Fanaticism as a phenomenon of compulsion is all of these: attempted breakout, fearful defense, self-gratification—and all of them simultaneously.

Our explanation is valid for very many cases. Nonetheless, it is not completely satisfactory. The active value-linkage of the "great" fanatics, discussed at length in the second chapter, points to backgrounds hardly to be seen as identical with the less conscious striving for mere self-gratification or self-assertion. In the case of the fanatics who see themselves obligated to a social, political, artistic, or religious value and who creatively cooperate in its formation, the imperative for an ultimate meaningfulness beyond all individual and unconscious striving for pleasure and self-assertion seems to be a codetermining factor. Frequently enough even this striving for meaningfulness may possibly be revealed as a "mask" of the aforementioned instincts; yet our discussions should have established the existence of an original and authentic striving for value-fulfillment and meaningfulness which compels the fullest use of all energies and this can also be combined with fanatic behavior.

Whenever a value is experienced as absolute and hence becomes a *fanum,* it is impossible for man to display an indifferent attitude toward it. Whenever one meets God "existentially" the distinction between freedom and coercion seems not too important: a highly involving "holy necessity" then determines one's activity and total vitality. The breakthrough into a higher realm of power as a rule causes the person in such situations to experience his own littleness and powerlessness and holds him in its unyielding grip. The person becomes a prisoner or even one possessed by the "daimonion." From an *external* psychological viewpoint such a being-gripped is scarcely distinguishable from the incubus of fanatic possession. But here the content is not a hitherto repressed and fearfully parried or camouflaged pleasure complex but a revelation that is at once pleasant and frightening in its effect: the numinous in its twofold aspect of the *fascinosum* and the *tremendum* stands before the person.

Rudolf Otto, the author of the well-known work *Das Heilige,* is not alone in his knowledge of such experiences. C. G. Jung's theory of the invasion of numinous powers out of the collective unconscious is both a significant and deliberate attempt to enclose in psychological formulations such experiences of his psychiatric work as well as his personal life. In many of these contents which at times come suddenly to the surface Jung recognizes the so-called "archetypal" figures and models which befall man not as the individual but simply as man. There are structurally grounded dispositions that bear within themselves not only the possibility and capacity but even the necessity of undergoing and forming such archetypal experiences. For Jung these archetypes are dominants of the psyche and their function is threefold: they are organizing factors which guarantee that certain

human and always necessary purposes and goals are
striven for; they are furthermore the great inspirers, per-
sistently urging toward new solutions and patternings;
and finally they function as bridges of meaning, dis-
closing the significance of the course of development at
each phase and in its entirety, that is, the interconnection
of individual and overlapping relationships.

In our context here there are two statements of Jung
which are especially important. One emphasizes the law
of an almost compelling course of opposition between
the conscious and the unconscious, the so-called *enantiodromia*. According to Jung, "the only person who
escapes the grim law of enantiodromia is the man who
knows how to separate himself from the unconscious,
not by repressing it—for then it simply attacks him from
the rear—but by putting it clearly before him as *that
which he is not*."[57] Jung understands some forms of psychic compulsion from the basis of this grim law. The
compulsion of the fanatic, too, can be postulated on the
one hand as a defense against the breakthrough of such
unconscious collective contents and on the other hand
also as a necessarily occurring invasion of these very
contents, which then break through every dam. For Jung
this is one of the fundamental laws he found repeatedly
confirmed by experience.

Jung's second statement explains why in some cases
the primordial images breaking out of the collective
unconscious lead astray to inhuman, cruel, and even

criminal impulses and actions. "The images contain not only all the fine and good things that humanity has ever thought and felt, but the worst infamies and devilries of which men have been capable. Owing to their specific energy—for they behave like highly charged autonomous centers of power—they exert a fascinating and possessive influence upon the conscious mind and can thus produce extensive alterations in the subject."[58] Whenever a compelling incursion of such collective contents takes place there is great danger that such an inflation simultaneously becomes an identification with these values and their double aspect. This then necessarily leads to the cramped compulsive attitude, which with a sense of mission fights for a value but in so doing can become inhuman and even criminal.

In concluding this chapter we must once more emphasize that our classification of pathological symptoms into definite syndromes should not be seen as comfortable labels. Our awareness of the wholeness of man, of the individual integration-coherence of all energies and functions does not permit one-sided approaches. Yet a manysided view of the particular aspects can sharpen the eye for certain specific forms and so lead to a better grasp of the total phenomenon.

Final Reflections

Our explanations have shown how erroneous it is to use the label "fanaticism" without more precise distinctions. This term is in need of clear differentiation if it is to be psychologically useful. The *multilayeredness* of the problem has become so clear that it is not feasible to reduce it to a single formula and to try to understand it only from the perspective of a specific life-project. Only he who is willing to see fanatic behavior in one instance as a peripheral phenomenon of a transitory mood and in another as a permanent core-formation due to disposition and development can approach the phenomenon of

fanaticism without prejudice. Moreover we must take
into account that it can be combined in many different
ways with external and internal value needs as well as
with environmental circumstances if we are gradually to
arrive at an adequate understanding of this intriguing
yet dangerous expression of an inner state of agitation
and of intensive behavior. This should firmly convince
us that a single method can never be adequate for viewing
such multilayered contexts and conditions, let alone for
bringing them into the horizon of understanding. It is
indeed the tragedy of a great portion of mankind's intellectual efforts that, leaping over the tension-polarity of
the concretely living, there is danger of falling into an
abstract monistic or dualistic system. Both these ways
of thinking are the very breeding ground of fanatic
behavior, for both try to avoid the serious task of understanding more deeply the concretely living in its counter-
tension and of bringing it into an ever new neutraliza-
tion.[1] Through a magic formula of simplification they
make it possible to subordinate the multilayered reality
to an unrestricted "efficiency." The efficiency principle
represses the reality principle, and fanaticism stands
knocking at the door.

Another thing that becomes clear from our discussion
is, as we have stressed in the introduction, the *actuality*
of the theme. This actuality through the very multiplicity
of the realms in which fanaticism ominously rages even
today has proved itself to be universal. Modern man,

like man of earlier phases of consciousness, still has the unrecognized yet stubborn tendency to absolute ideas and isolated individual values. No less than the man of earlier cultures he employs magical practices, rationalizing and concealing them behind the magic of a certain, seemingly legitimate *fanum*. At times this *fanum* is something quite grossly primitive, hypnotically induced on man by advertising methods employing the help of mass media and even the psychology of the unconscious. It seductively promises ultimate and supreme fulfillment. Even though we have illustrated our discussions mainly by personages and events of the past it should not be too difficult to show that many ideologies of the present manifested in politics, art, social life, and in certain religious phenomena are typically fanatic. We are witnesses of a deliberately instigated and ideologically abused race fanaticism which leads constantly to unrest and bloody clashes; we also experience periodical episodes of hysterical mass fanaticism artificially produced by experts—for example during presidential elections—and we feel the effects of a "scientifically" manipulated propaganda, presenting banalities as absolute needs and, through constant repetitions, endowing them with a compulsive character, whereas only yesterday no one had an inkling of their possibility. Consequently we experience the fanatic effects of multifarious addictions on our instinctually driven adolescents: cars, TV, and so forth.

In spite of all the official slogans of "objectivity,"

tolerance, and patience, we thus (perhaps according to the law of "countercourse") encounter time and again a form of fanaticism quite adept in electrifying the indolent masses. The weeds of fanaticism thrive in every fertile field of human culture and can never be completely eradicated. Thus the problem of fanaticism will always be topic. These facts not only give us the right but even compel us to see the phenomenon of fanaticism primarily as a *psychic problem*. The human psyche itself bears within it this capability of fanaticism and demonstrates a fatal tendency to realize this possibility ever anew. Even in the religions and various denominations which proclaim the commandment of love as the supreme and decisive good, at the side of the psychically well-balanced representative is the fanatic type who does not feel right when he cannot explode in an unrestrained way or when he does not succeed in making his unrest the sole salvation recipe for a multitude of disciples. Even well-established and superior forms of man's spirituality and ideology often find it difficult to resist these dynamic instigators (even when their program is not progressive). The compensatory character of most fanatic behavior shows only too clearly that these zealots lack the psychic equilibrium grounded in a gradually developed core of the person, which is not to be confused with the metaphysical concept of personality.

It may come as a surprise that in the course of our deliberations we have offered no hints for a "treatment" of fanatics. And yet our very insight into the complexity of fanatic behavior and forms of expression, and even more our recognition of its many possible backgrounds, should make us cautious regarding any overhasty therapeutic recommendations. In any case, the possibility of a psychic underground must be kept in mind. But over and beyond this it should have become clear that in some cases the analytic treatment can be indicated even though the difficulty of this method of treatment should not be overlooked, especially when dealing with fanatics of an inner and authentic value attitude. An awareness of the multilayered nature of the problem will be a very valuable help, especially for the analytical method of treatment.

It is even more important to give full attention to the *prophylaxis*. In the realm of adult education mass media should not mix together undifferentiated banalities with essentials to such a degree that hierarchies of value and rank are left opaque, nor should they be centralized to such a degree that some day they can be abused as instruments of a single party. Furthermore there must be a methodical education of the truly pliable youth toward tolerance in the sense of spiritual breadth. This will be possible only if the actual problems are consciously delineated in their historical and ideological perspective so that the different attempts at solution lead to a true insight into the backgrounds. Only an open, questioning attitude as the principle means of education toward the capability of value experience can guarantee the gradual disappearance of narrow-mindedness and hardened fixations. It is only in this way, too, that deathly boredom can be banished from the realm of education, a boredom which with an inner lawfulness provokes outbreaks of unrestrained intensity. Fanaticism can be overcome only through something more convincing and more truly living than fanaticism itself.

Notes

INTRODUCTION

[1] Cf. Georg Dehio, *Das Strassburger Münster* (Munich, 1922), p. 27.

[2] C. G. Jung, *Two Essays on Analytical Psychology* (New York: Meridian, 1956), p. 81.

[3] W. Horstmann, "Fanatismus—Aberglaube—Wahnvorstellung," in *Zeitschrift für die gesamte Neurologie und Psychiatrie,* 1910, p. 216.

[4] Gerhardt Pfahler, *Der Mensch und sein Lebenswerkzeug; Erbcharakterologie* (Stuttgart: E. Klett, 1954), p. 323.

[5] The so-called probabilism dispute began about 1580 (Bartholomäus de Medina, O.P.) and was the concern of the moralists during two entire centuries (up to Alphonsus Liguori, d. 1762). Cf. Denzinger-Umberg, *Enchiridion Symbolorum* 18–20 (1932), no. 1151 ff.; 1219.

[6] Here we deliberately ignore the usual definitions of fanaticism, since they almost always emphasize only a single aspect without taking into consideration the multiplicity of kinds of fanatic behavior.

[7] Cf. P. Lersch, *Der Aufbau des Charakters* (Leipzig: Barth, 1938), pp. 4–5.

⁸ Cf. Igor Caruso's concept of neurosis: *Existential Psychology: From Analysis to Synthesis* (New York: Herder and Herder, 1964), and *Bios, Psyche, Person* (Freiburg: Alber, 1957).

⁹ WW Naumann, Bd. XI, p. 408. We found this cited in: Kesselring, *Nietzsche und sein Zarathustra in psychiatrischer Beleuchtung* (Affoltern: Aehren-Verlag, 1954), p. 22. Kesselring adds: "Unfortunately this informative quotation has been omitted by the Nietzsche archive in all smaller editions; not even the official N-register, edited by R. Öhler, contains an allusion to this fanaticism."

CHAPTER ONE:
FANATICISM AS A PROBLEM OF INTENSITY

¹ In this context we refer to Albert Wellek's interesting discussions of intensity and depth in his book *Die Polarität im Aufbau des Charakters* (Bern: A Francke, 1950).

² Wilhelm Lange, *Genie, Irrsinn und Ruhm* (Munich: E. Reinhardt, 1956), pp. 315–320.

³ Georg Stertz, "Verschrobene Fanatiker" in *Berliner klinische Wochenschrift,* 1919, p. 587.

⁴ G. Kujath, "Über religiösen Fanatismus" in *Allgemeine Zeitschrift für Psychiatrie und ihre Grenzgebiete,* 1942, Bd. 120, p. 67 ff.

⁵ Walter Muschg, *Tragische Literaturgeschichte* (Bern: Francke, 1953), p. 641.

⁶ E. Nolde, *Das eigene Leben,* cited in W. Winkler, *Psychologie der modernen Kunst* (Tübingen: Alma Mater Verlag, 1949), p. 54.

⁷ Ibid.

⁸ Ludwig Pastor, *Geschichte der Päpste* (Freiburg im

Breisgau, 1891), III/1, p. 492, footnote 3 (available in English as *History of the Popes* [London: Hodges, 1891]).

[9] Ibid., p. 481, footnote 2.

[10] Oskar Pfister, *Christianity and Fear* (London: Allen & Unwin, 1948), p. 433.

[11] Nicola Sementovsky-Kurilo, *Savonarola; Revolutionär, Ketzer oder Prophet?* (Olten: Walter, 1950), pp. 101, 171.

[12] Ronald A. Knox, *Enthusiasm* (Oxford: Clarendon Press, 1950), p. 377. Knox is quoting from L. Figuier as quoted in P. F. Mathieu, *Histoire des miraculés et des convulsionnaires de Saint-Médard* (Paris, 1864), p. 217, and also from Grégoire, *Histoire des sectes religieuses* (1829), II, 130, and *Mémoires pour servir à l'histoire ecclésiastique pendant le XVIIIème siècle* (Bruges, 1825), II, 44.

[13] Wellek, pp. 117–118.

[14] Gerhardt Pfahler, *Der Mensch und sein Lebenswerkzeug: Erbcharakterologie* (Stuttgart: E. Klett, 1954), p. 108.

[15] Sementovsky, p. 164.

[16] *Thomas Müntzer, sein Leben und seine Schriften,* ed. Brandt, cited in Walter Nigg, *Das Buch der Ketzer* (Zurich: Artemis, 1949), p. 352 ff.

[17] Alexander von Muralt, *Wahnsinniger oder Prophet? Darstellung und Diskussion eines mit Psychotherapie behandelten Falles von Gottesdienststörung* (Zurich: Europa-Verlag, 1946), p. 26.

[18] Cited by Miller de la Fuente, "Fanatismus, ein Symptom der Minderwertigkeit," *Deutsche Medizin,* LVI, no. 33 (1930), p. 1402.

[19] Nigg, p. 372 ff.

[20] Pfahler, p. 108.

[21] Wellek, p. 118.

[22] Kujath, p. 73.

[23] Ernst Kretschmer, *Physique and Character,* (London: Kegan Paul, Trench, Trubner, 1936), p. 156.

[24] Ibid., p. 183.

[25] W. Horstmann, "Fanatismus-Aberglaube-Wahnvorstellung," in *Zeitschrift für die gesamte Neurologie und Psychiatrie,* 1910, p. 216.

[26] Cf. S. Streicher, *Die Tragödie einer Gottsucherin* (Einsiedeln: Aust, 1945).

[27] Hans Kunz, *Die Aggressivität und die Zärtlichkeit* (Bern: Francke, 1946).

[28] Quoted by Josef Pieper, *Fortitude and Temperance* (New York: Pantheon, 1954), p. 104.

[29] C. G. Jung, *Psychological Types* (New York: Harcourt, Brace, 1926), p. 492.

[30] René Fülöp-Miller, *Lenin und Gandhi* (Zurich: Amalthea-Verlag, 1927), p. 26 (available in English as *Lenin and Ghandhi* [London: Putnam, 1927]).

[31] Ludwig Klages, *Die Grundlagen der Charakterkunde* (Leipzig: Barth, 1936), p. 193.

[32] Kretschmer, *Physique and Character,* p. 255.

[33] Ibid., pp. 254–255.

[34] Ernst Kretschmer, *Geniale Menschen,* 4th ed. (Berlin, 1948), p. 25 (available in English as *The Psychology of Men of Genius* [London: Kegan Paul, Trench, Trubner, 1931]).

[35] Sementovsky, p. 184.

[36] Kretschmer, *Geniale Menschen,* p. 24.

[37] Savonarola, *Auswahl aus seinen Schriften und Predigten,* translated into German by J. Schnitzer (1928), p. 230.

[38] Pastor, III/1, p. 472.

[39] Oskar Pfister, *Calvins Eingreifen in die Hexenprozesse von Peney* (Zurich: Artemis, 1947), p. 33.

[40] Cf. Nigg, p. 357.

[41] Quoted in Fülöp-Miller, p. 120.

[42] In *Magie des Extrêmes; les études Carmélitaines* (Bruges: Desclée de Brouwer, 1952), p. 64.

[43] Horstmann, p. 220 ff.

[44] Especially in respect to radioactivity, according to a report published in *Münchner Medizinischen Klinik,* "in the Anglo-Saxon states it has been observed that persons who came in direct contact with radioactive materials after some time manifested character defects which had not previously existed; these individuals became cantankerous, irascible and discontented and found themselves in conflict with their surroundings." Professor Hans Thirring, skeptical of this report, had to admit that also in the institute of radiology in Vienna, influences on the psyche have been noticed "but substantially less frequently and in no case to such a serious degree as reported in the cases of England and America," and that the effects were in opposite directions. "For while one of the scientists became irritable, intolerant and aggressive through the effect of radiation . . . the other displayed a kind of jolly mood which was in clear contrast to his otherwise definitely taciturn and humorless temperament" ("Charakter-änderung durch Radioaktivität" in *Weltwoche,* August 21, 1953).

[45] Aleks. Pontvik, *Heilen durch Musik* (Zurich: Rascher, 1955), p. 26.

[46] David Hart, *Der tiefenpsychologische Begriff der Kompensation* (Zurich: Origo-Verlag, 1956), p. 191.

[47] Statements of C. G. Jung in a personal conversation with the author.

[48] Savonarola, *Auswahl aus seinen Schriften und Predigten,* pp. 231–244.

[49] A. Vierkandt, "Ursprünge und Gefahren des Fanatis-

mus" in *Die Hilfe, Zeitschrift für Politik, Wirtschaft und geistige Bewegung,* XLVII, no. 19 (1941), p. 289 ff.

[50] Stertz, p. 588.

[51] Miller de la Fuente, p. 1402.

[52] Kujath, p. 74.

[53] Regarding Caruso, cf. our Introduction, footnote 8.

[54] Cf. Pfister, *Christianity and Fear.*

[55] Cf. Jacques Madaule, *Le drame albigeois et le destin français,* (Paris: Grasset, 1962).

[56] C. G. Jung, *Two Essays on Analytical Psychology,* p. 81.

CHAPTER TWO:
FANATICISM AS A PROBLEM OF VALUE-ATTITUDE

[1] Georg Stertz, "Verschrobene Fanatiker," *Berliner klinische Wochenschrift,* 1919, p. 588.

[2] Eduard Spranger, *Lebensformen,* 6th ed. (Halle: Niemeyer, 1927), pp. 121–236 (available in English as *Types of Men* [Halle: Niemeyer, 1928]).

[3] *Philosophisches Wörterbuch* (Freiburg: Herder, 1948), p. 410.

[4] Cf. Igor Caruso, *Existential Psychology: From Analysis to Synthesis* (New York: Herder and Herder, 1964).

[5] Cf. C. G. Jung, *Über psychische Energetik und das Wesen der Träume* (Zürich, 1948), pp. 121–143, "Allgemeines zur Komplextheorie"; and Jolande Jacobi, *Complex, Archetype, Symbol* (New York: Pantheon, 1959), pp. 6–30.

[6] C. G. Jung, *Two Essays on Analytical Psychology* (New York: Meridian, 1956), p. 81.

[7] Eugen Kogon, *Der SS-Staat* (Munich: Alber, 1946), p. 287 (English adaptation: *The Theory and Practice of Hell* [New York: Berkley, 1958]).

[8] Ibid., p. 299.

[9] Adolf Eichmann, tape recording used at the trial. Cf. *Neue Zürcher Zeitung,* April 22, 1961, no. 1498, Blatt 2.

[10] Colin Wilson, *The Outsider* (Boston: Houghton Mifflin, 1956), pp. 168–169.

[11] Cf. Josef Pieper, *Über das Schweigen Goethes* (Munich: Kösel, 1951).

[12] The dancer is an especially clear example of the distinction between the pure form-perfectionist and the creative molder of an idea. Harald Kreutzberg, for instance, is not so much interested in the dance as such; rather he dances ideas, for example: the exorcism of devils, and myth of Orpheus, Job's rebellion and devotion, the song of the night. Nijinsky sought an even more profound meaning and value in the dance; for him it was basically transformation of one's being: he became what he danced. In ecstatic intoxication he experienced the expansion of his own being: "I am God" is bursting out of him. Hereby levels of experience are achieved and striven for which the mere form-perfectionist does not attempt to achieve and to suffer through. But at the same time these examples clearly show that there are many intermediate stages between the pure form-fanatic and the fanatic of inner content.

[13] Cf. Walter Winkler, *Psychologie der modernen Kunst* (Tübingen, 1949), pp. 73–81; and Neue Zürcher Zeitung, March 6, 1965, "Dichtung als Sprache."

[14-17] Cf. Winkler, pp. 153, 170, 177.

[18] Cf. Arthur Koestler *et al., The God That Failed,* ed. R. H. S. Crossman (New York: Harper, 1949).

[19] Gustav Landauer, *Aufruf zum Sozialismus* (Berlin, 1919), p. 34; quoted in Spranger, p. 178.

[20] Winkler, p. 135.

[21] Ibid.

[22] Josef Rudin, *Psychotherapy and Religion* (Notre Dame, Ind.: University of Notre Dame Press, 1967), pp. 206–215.

[23] Henrik Ibsen, *Brand,* trans. C. H. Herford, in *Collected Works,* III (New York: Scribner's, 1928), 22–23.

[24] Ernst Kretschmer, *Geniale Menschen,* 4th ed. (Berlin, 1948), p. 24.

[25] Cf. Rudin, *Psychotherapy and Religion,* pp. 155–162.

[26] Quoted in David Hart, *Der tiefenpsychologische Begriff der Kompensation* (Zurich: Origo-Verlag, 1956), p. 10.

[27] *Psyche,* July, 1954, p. 67.

[28] Cf. Josef Rudin, *Der Erlebnisdrang* (Lucerne, 1942), pp. 68–74.

[29] Cf. C. G. Jung, "On the Relation of Analytical Psychology to the Poetic Art," *The Spirit in Man, Art, and Literature (Collected Works,* Bollingen Series XX [Princeton, N. J.], vol. 15, 1966), 65–83.

[30] Julius Bahle, *Der musikalische Schaffensprozess* (Leipzig: Hirzel, 1936), I, 242.

[31] Cf. Rudin, *Der Erlebnisdrang,* p. 66.

[32] Ibid., p. 89.

[33] In regard to the problem of the genius, cf. Wilhelm Lange, *Genie, Irrsinn und Ruhm* (Munich: E. Reinhardt, 1956).

[34] Even if one does not wish to view Kierkegaard as a fanatic, a fanatic trend is not to be overlooked, especially in his last essays, *The Moment.*

[35] The following quotations are taken from: *The Complete Letters of Van Gogh,* 3 vols. (Greenwich, Conn.: New York Graphic Society, 1958).

[36] Cf. Lange, pp. 308–310.

[37] Stertz, p. 588.

[38] G. Kujath, "Über religiösen Fanatismus," *Allgemeine*

Zeitschrift für Psychiatrie und ihre Grenzgebiete, 1942, Bd. 120, p. 15.

[39] Bahle, I, 174–175.

[40] Cf. our Chapter Three: "Pathology of Fanaticism."

[41] Cf. Hart.

[42] Lange, p. 275.

[43] Alexander von Muralt, *Wahnsinniger oder Prophet?* (Zurich: Europa-Verlag, 1946), pp. 10, 14, 16, 19.

[44] *The Complete Letters of Van Gogh,* III, 25.

[45] *Neue Zürcher Zeitung,* November 19, 1955, "Militärdienstverweigerung aus Gewissensgründen."

[46] Heinz Zwicker, *Seelisches Leiden und schöpferische Leistung,* (Bern: Haupt, 1954), p. 35.

[47] Ibid., p. 34.

[48] Lange, p. 363.

[49] Bernhard Welte, *Vom Wesen und Unwesen der Religion* (Frankfurt/Main: Knecht, 1952).

[50] C. G. Jung, *Über psychische Energetik und das Wesen der Träume,* 2nd ed. (Zurch, 1948) p. 219; *Development of Personality* (*Collected Works,* Bollingen Series XX, vol. 17, 1954); Psychological Types (New York: Harcourt, Brace, 1926).

[51] Quoted in Lange, p. 445.

CHAPTER THREE:
THE PATHOLOGY OF FANATICISM

[1] W. Horstmann, "Fanatismus-Aberglaube-Wahnvorstellung," *Zeitschrift für die gesamte Neurologie und Psychiatrie,* 1910, p. 218.

[2] Kurt Schneider, *Psychopathic Personalities* (London: Cassell, 1958), p. ix.

[3] Ibid., p. 3.

[4] Ibid., p. 5.

[5] Kurt Schneider, "Kritik der klinisch-typologischen Psychopathenbetrachtung," *Der Nervenarzt,* XIX (1948), p. 9.

[6] Schneider, *Psychopathic Personalities,* p. 98.

[7] Ibid., p. 99.

[8] Ibid., p. 101.

[9] Ibid., p. 8.

[10] Georg Stertz, "Verschrobene Fanatiker," *Berliner klinische Wochenschrift,* 1919, p. 588.

[11] Ibid., p. 587.

[12] Horstmann, p. 255.

[13] Wilhelm Heinen, "Rigorismus in der Pastoral," *Anima,* XI (1956), I., pp. 80–81.

[14] Ernst Kretschmer, *Geniale Menschen,* 4th ed. (Berlin, 1948), p. 8.

[15] Miller de la Fuente, "Fanatismus, ein Symptom der Minderwertigkeit," *Deutsche Medizin,* LVI, no. 33 (1930), p. 1402 ff.

[16] Cf. *Neue Zürcher Zeitung,* May 25, 1965, I. "Das Verbrechertum der SS."

[17] Alexander von Muralt, *Wahnsinniger oder Prophet?* (Zurich, Europa-Verlag, 1946), p. 46.

[18] In respect to the *puer aeternus,* cf. M. L. Franz, in Bruno Goetz, *Reich ohne Raum* (1962).

[19] Cf. pp. 28–29.

[20] Henry Charles Lea, *A History of the Inquisition of Spain,* 4 vols. (New York: Macmillan, 1922), III, 225, 227, 228.

[21] Birger Dahlerus, *The Last Attempt* (London, 1948), pp. 119–120, quoted in Alan Bullock, *Hitler: A Study in Tyranny,* rev. ed. (New York: Harper, 1962), p. 548.

[22] Von Muralt, p. 22.

[23] G. Kujath, "Über religiösen Fanatismus," *Allgemeine Zeitschrift für Psychiatrie und ihre Grenzgebiete,* 1942, Bd. 120, p. 70 ff.

[24] Ernst Kretschmer, *Physique and Character* (London: Kegan Paul, Trench, Trubner, 1936).

[25] Kujath, p. 72.

[26] R. Fülöp-Miller, *Lenin und Gandhi* (Zurich: Amalthea-Verlag, 1927), pp. 26–27.

[27] Bullock, pp. 406–407.

[28] N. D. (Nuremberg Documents) 3,569-PS, quoted in Bullock, pp. 794–795.

[29] Bullock, p. 793.

[30] Josef Rudin, *Psychotherapy and Religion* (Notre Dame, Ind.: University of Notre Dame Press, 1967), p. 43 ff.

[31] *Neue Zürcher Zeitung,* February 13, 1965.

[32] C. J. Burckhardt, *Meine Danziger Mission, 1937–1939* (DTV, 1962), p. 109.

[33] Kujath, p. 73.

[34] Stertz, p. 588.

[35] Horstmann, p. 225.

[36] Schneider, *Psychopathic Personalities,* pp. 99, 101.

[37] Cf. Kretschmer, *Physique and Character.*

[38] Cf. Oskar Pfister, *Christianity and Fear* (London: Allen & Unwin, 1948).

[39] Savonarola, *Auswahl aus seinen Schriften und Predigten,* trans. J. Schnitzer (1928), p. 238.

[40] A. Favre-Dorsaz, *Calvin et Loyola, deux réformes* (Paris: Editions Universitaires, 1951), p. 97.

[41] J. Schnitzer, trans., *Auswahl aus seinen Schriften und Predigten,* by Savonarola, p. vii.

the happy, balanced temperament" (*Der Nervenartz,* XIX
(1948), p. 7). About the hyperthymic psychopath he says:
"With the hyperthymic and also with the very active psychopath we mean the extreme of personalities with a happy basic
frame of mind, a vivacious (sanguine) temperament and a
certain activism" (Schneider, *Klinische Psychopathologie*
4th ed. [Stuttgart: Thieme, 1955], p. 26).

[56] Hans Kunz, *Die Aggressivität und die Zärtlichkeit* (Bern: A. Francke, 1946), p. 49.

[57] C. G. Jung, *Two Essays on Analytical Psychology* (New York, Meridian, 1956), p. 83.

[58] Ibid., p. 80.

FINAL REFLECTIONS

[1] Cf. Romano Guardini, *Der Gegensatz; Versuch einer Philosophie des Lebendig-Konkreten* (Mainz: Matthias Grünewald Verlag, 1925).

Index